Spectres of Pessimism

Mark Schmitt

Spectres of Pessimism

A Cultural Logic of the Worst

Mark Schmitt
Department of Cultural Studies
TU Dortmund University
Dortmund, Germany

ISBN 978-3-031-25350-8   ISBN 978-3-031-25351-5   (eBook)
https://doi.org/10.1007/978-3-031-25351-5

This Palgrave Macmillan imprint is published by the registered company Springer Nature
Switzerland AG.
The registered company address is: Gewerbestrasse 11, 6330 Cham, Switzerland

Acknowledgements

This book could not have been written without the support of friends, family, colleagues, students and institutions. I would like to thank my colleagues at TU Dortmund University for providing an inspiring work environment. Marie Hologa, David Kerler, Christian Lenz, Sophia Möllers, Sarah Neef, Cyprian Piskurek, Gerold Sedlmayr and the participants of the colloquium "Literary and Cultural Theory" provided feedback on early drafts. Ronja Niemczik kindly helped with library research. I am grateful to the students in my seminars "Pessimism", "Britain's Futures", "Precarious Temporalities" and "Ahuman Futures" for inspiring discussions and for allowing me to test chapter ideas. Ideas for this book have been presented at conferences in Dresden, Essen, Falmouth, Lisbon, London and Mainz. My thanks to all organisers and participants for their feedback and questions.

This book is a major result of my research during a fellowship granted by the Stuart Hall Foundation (2016–2019). I would particularly like to thank the trustees Catherine Hall, Gregor McLennan and Michael Rustin for providing this opportunity and for their encouragement.

I am grateful to friends and colleagues who have provided feedback on chapter drafts, collaborated on related projects and engaged in conversations about the worst: Florian Cord, Sandra Danneil, Ariane de Waal, Kai Fischer, Niall Griffiths, Kieran Harrington, Shona Hunter, Laurence Kane, Evangelia Kindinger, Tammy Kirchner, Solvejg Nitzke, Sarah Reininghaus, Anika Simon and Andreas Warneke.

At Palgrave, I would like to thank Amy Invernizzi for reaching out and supporting the project, and Chandralekha Mahamel Raja for coordination and support. I would also like to thank the anonymous peer reviewers for their comments and suggestions.

Finally, my heartfelt personal thanks to my friends and the extended Schmitt family for their support.

About This Book

This book argues that that philosophical pessimism can offer vital impulses for contemporary cultural studies. This book explores the emergence of new pessimisms that speak to the political, social, cultural and ecological crises of the present, including ecological pessimism, queer pessimism, reproductive pessimism and afropessimism. If cultural studies want to critically assess the cultural logic of the worst that characterises the current conjuncture and contribute to a critical analysis of temporality and prefigurative thought, they must take on the philosophical challenge of the spectres of pessimism haunting thought, affect and cultural representations.

This Pivot

- Offers original readings of pessimist philosophies and provides an introduction to new pessimisms, including afropessimism, queer and reproductive pessimism and ecological pessimism.
- Combines pessimist philosophy and hauntology to offer new impulses for cultural studies.
- Reassesses utopianism in the context of cultural theory.
- Uses pessimism, utopianism and hauntology for an analytical framework to read a diverse range of literary texts and films.
- Addresses scholars, students and general readers interested in philosophy, cultural theory, futures studies and literary and film studies.

CONTENTS

CHAPTER 1

Introduction: "Being for Being Against": Pessimism and the Cultural Moment

Abstract Pessimism, both in philosophical thought and in everyday affective, political and cultural life, is persistent and ubiquitous. From the climate crisis and global pandemic to the chronic multiple crises of capitalism and politics revolving around identity-based discrimination, there seems plenty to be pessimistic about. Pessimism has found diverse forms of philosophical and cultural expression, and it is the latter that this book will primarily be concerned with. Pessimism poses a challenge to dominant notions of temporality and progress—aspects that it shares with hauntological thought. In Jacques Derrida and Mark Fisher's theories of hauntology, the present is disrupted by hauntings from the political and cultural past and potential futures. Likewise, pessimism haunts contemporary culture and fundamentally unsettles linear temporalities. The introduction summarises and systematises various expressions of what this book proposes to call new pessimisms. These include apocalyptic/dystopian fictions, new cultural pessimism, queer pessimism and afropessimism, among others. Informed by Stuart Hall and Lawrence Grossberg's work, the introduction proposes the method of conjunctural analysis to address the current spectres of pessimism. The introductory chapter offers a model analysis of a central conjunctural text representative of the current pessimist moment, Hari Kunzru's novel *Red Pill* (2020).

Keywords Pessimism • Afropessimism • Queer pessimism • Ecological pessimism • Conjunctural analysis • Affect • Negativity • Modernity • Future • Temporality • Hauntology • Hari Kunzru

A New Pessimism

If the Deloitte Global 2021 Millennial and Gen Z Survey is anything to go by, we are living in bleak times—an age of "absolute pessimism".[1] The professional services network surveyed the attitudes of the two youngest generations currently entering the job market. While the survey testifies to the increasing awareness for social, political and ecological responsibility in these generations, it also states that "[o]ptimism reaches nadir": Millennials and Gen Z are among the most hopeless and anxious generations, with "pessimism about social/political climates" reaching "historic levels".[2] Taken in the second year of the COVID-19 pandemic, the survey reflects young people's reactions to a global state of exception, but also attitudes and tendencies that go beyond the present moment. The impact of the international response to the antiracist movement Black Lives Matter, the antisexist movement #MeToo, but also the long-term impact of environmental issues and the instability of economic markets factor into responses to the survey. Mental health emerges as a central aspect in the survey and demonstrates the correlation of personal subjective aspects and the global, long-term situation.

The Deloitte survey conveys a profound sense of uncertainty and insecurity in young people's subjective experience of temporality and the current historical moment. It seems as if the twenty-first century confirms the "collapse of the future" that the Italian philosopher Franco Berardi diagnosed the twentieth century with.[3] The survey thus characterises the current conjuncture. In cultural studies, a conjuncture is the "description of a social formation as fractured and conflictual, along multiple axes, planes, and scales, constantly in search of temporary balances or structural stabilities through a variety of practices and processes of struggle and negation".[4] A conjunctural analysis in the cultural studies tradition is concerned with these complex and often ambiguous processes that amount to the interplay of political, social and economic structures, the cultural expressions and the dominant affects of a historical conjuncture.

This book argues that the current conjuncture is marked by a cultural logic of the worst. It is marked by a sense of the "future as endtimes",[5]

which is symptomatic of a temporality that has become increasingly precarious. Within this logic, it is not just the prospect of an uncertain and dangerous future that induces anxiety; rather, the conjunctural pessimism is characteristic of a moment in which "[t]he real object of [...] anxiety is time itself, not merely in the sense that the present has become strange, but that time itself has become strange".[6] A conjunctural analysis therefore must extend to pessimism in its diverse and ambivalent expressions, as a philosophy, a prognostic perspective on the future, a political stance and an affect.

Pessimism, both in philosophical thought and in everyday affective, political and cultural life, is notoriously hard to grasp. Philosopher Eugene Thacker points out that it is difficult to systematically come to terms with something that is by many decried as merely a "bad attitude": "No one ever needs pessimism".[7] Yet, as the Deloitte survey demonstrates, pessimism is persistent and ubiquitous. From climate crisis and global pandemic to the chronic multiple crises of capitalism and the politics revolving around identity-based discrimination, there seems plenty to be pessimistic about. In the past two decades, a wealth of intellectual approaches has emerged that reflect this tendency which I would classify as "new" pessimisms. These pessimisms are new in that they forge perspectives that are suited to a diverse range of cultural issues and groups that characterise the contemporary world. They "particularize the universal truth of suffering"[8] and use this as a tool for epistemology, interrogation and critique in their respective specialised and marginalised areas.

For instance, Sara Ahmed proposes a queer pessimism in *The Promise of Happiness* (2010)—an approach that could also be used to label J. Jack Halberstam's *The Queer Art of Failure* (2011) and the earlier *No Future* by Lee Edelman (2004). In the context of race and ethnicity, afropessimism has emerged as a provocative perspective to tackle racism and racial identity constructions, with Frank B. Wilderson III's *Afropessimism* (2020) being the most recent and profound statement on the matter. Queer pessimism and afropessimism share their disruptive approach to the discourse of cultural constructions of identity—arguably one of the most urgent conflict zones of the contemporary moment. No less urgent are the recent pessimist interventions in ecological thought. Timothy Morton's *Dark Ecology* (2016) rethinks species belonging in the face of ecological crisis, drawing on the dark side of thought, from melancholy to negativity and the uncanny, to de-centre anthropocentric perspectives. Even more radically, Patricia MacCormack's *Ahuman Manifesto* (2020) calls for the "end of the Anthropocene" through veganism, antinatalism and welcoming human extinction through death activism. Even though MacCormack declares that her take is not pessimistic (she even disparages "white male angst pessimists who seek to enhance the reputation of pessimism"—a sideswipe against a lot of names which can be found in the present book),[9] but rather an affirmation of humanity's end for the sake of other species, her fundamentally misanthropic perspective can be placed alongside similar approaches such as David Benatar's outspokenly pessimist argument for antinatalism in *Better Never to Have Been* (2006) and *The Human Predicament* (2013).

While approaches like queer pessimism and afropessimism—what Packer and Stoneman call "micro-pessimisms"[10]—are concerned with the particulars of identity, these ecological and ahuman pessimisms transcend and de-centre the human, pointing to interspecies relations and ahuman contexts. This perspective beyond the human is also the focus of Eugene Thacker's writings, which probably are the most exhaustive contemporary exploration of the history and trajectories of pessimism, from his trilogy *The Horror of Philosophy* (2011–2015) to his *Cosmic Pessimism* (2015) and *Infinite Resignation* (2018) as well as his edition of the writings of Arthur Schopenhauer, *On the Suffering of the World* (2020). Thacker's cosmic pessimism is aimed at figuring a "world-without-us", a "spectral and speculative world" that allows humans to think of the world with human beings as not only de-centred, but subtracted from it.[11] This is a pessimist approach rooted as much in Schopenhauer's metaphysical pessimism as in the cosmic horror of weird fiction writer H. P. Lovecraft.[12] It is close to another cosmic pessimist (and horror writer), Thomas Ligotti, whose *The Conspiracy Against the Human Race: A Contrivance of Horror* (2010) pursues a similar approach in restoring a lineage of pessimist thought since Schopenhauer.

Both Thacker and Ligotti can hardly be called writers of popular appeal, but coincidentally they received some recognition when Nic Pizzolatto made it known that their work inspired him to write the infamously gloomy monologues of Rust Cohle, the main character of the first season of his hit TV show *True Detective* (2014). Through Rust Cohle, who explicitly refers to himself as a philosophical pessimist who is "bad at parties", then, pessimist attitudes were able to reach an audience that Ligotti and other pessimist writers would never be able to appeal to. As Joseph Packer and Ethan Stoneman have demonstrated in their analysis of *True

Detective, it is through careful packaging of form and content in the rhetoric and mode of genre entertainment that Pizzolatto's show manages to communicate its pessimistic worldview.[13] It is symptomatic of the current cultural logic of the worst that obscure pessimist thinkers would, as it were, poison the well of popular culture.

As an affective disposition and a philosophical position, pessimism haunts contemporary culture. Public intellectuals champion pessimism from opposing political angles: Slavoj Žižek's Marxist pessimism in *The Courage of Hopelessness* (2017) offers radical ideas to address late-stage capitalism while Roger Scruton identifies *The Uses of Pessimism* (2010) for what he claims to be a moderate realism beyond left- or right-wing ideologies when in fact it wears its unabashed conservatism on its sleeve in its constant polemics against anything that Scruton considers to be "postmodern" (ironically including the pessimists Theodor Adorno and Max Horkheimer). Even the self-help segment of the publishing market is not safe from pessimism's grasp: Arthur Schopenhauer and other philosophical miserabilists have found an unlikely second life in the eudaemonic promises of Mark Manson's popular anti-self-help books *The Subtle Art of Not Giving a Fuck: A Counterintuitive Approach to Living a Good Life* (2016) and *Everything Is Fucked: A Book about Hope* (2019) and German journalist Juliane Marie Schreiber's "rebellion against the terror of positivity" in her book *Ich möchte lieber nicht* ("I Would Prefer Not to") (2022). Such approaches could be termed lifestyle pessimism—a pessimism that might "risk being optimistic about pessimism itself".[14] This is a pessimism that claims to really just be a more realist perspective that ultimately helps you reach your goals and appreciate life. A more rigorous cosmic and metaphysical pessimism as practiced by the likes of Thomas Ligotti and Eugene Thacker, however, makes no such promises.

It is primarily the cultural expressions of pessimism that the present book will be concerned with. The book traces strands of pessimism in cultural theory as well as in cultural production, such as in literature and film, and argues that pessimism is an integral part of the conjuncture's prevailing negative affect towards the future, a "being for being against".[15] A similar cultural studies approach has been proposed in earlier books on pessimism by Ian Bailey and Oliver Bennett.[16] Joshua Foa Dienstag criticised the latter for the use of Raymond Williams' concept of the structure of feeling, a central concept of early cultural studies, for blurring the "distinction between pessimism as emotion and as theory in a way that I believe is counterproductive for understanding the philosophical lineage I explore here".[17] For Dienstag, it is important to separate pessimism as a body of thought from a mental and affective disposition since equating pessimism with disposition is often used to delegitimise its intellectual, philosophical and political validity. As Dienstag argues, "theories of progress are not the same thing as a cheerful attitude toward life", and therefore, pessimism should be allowed to be judged on similar grounds.[18]

While I wholeheartedly agree with Dienstag that it is necessary to separate pessimism as a theory from a mental disposition in order to isolate it as a body of ideas for political theory and as a philosophy (even if it is "antisystematic"[19]), I would argue that it is still necessary to acknowledge the affective-emotional component of pessimism in order to do it justice. It is becoming increasingly difficult to completely divorce it from emotion and affect, especially when pessimism's place in a wider cultural field is taken into consideration. As the Deloitte survey demonstrates, pessimism has arrived in public discourse precisely as an affective and emotional disposition, grounded in a prognostic assessment of present-day realities. Even though one could argue that it is possible to adopt different epistemological approaches to what triggers young people's pessimism, it is hard to dismiss the affective reality of such sentiments. These are grounded, I contend, in a more complex conjunctural pattern, and taking pessimism seriously as both an affective disposition and a viable theoretical approach does not only have to be mutually exclusive—it can also help us to develop a more nuanced and accurate assessment of what I call the current cultural logic of the worst.

I base my approach to conjunctural analysis on Lawrence Grossberg's modification of Stuart Hall and Antonio Gramsci's theorisations of conjuncture: "It is the complex product of multiple lines of force, determination, and resistance, with different temporalities and spatialities. Yet, a conjuncture has to be constructed, narrated, fabricated."[20] Conjunctural analysis, then,

> can be broadly defined as the analysis of convergent and divergent tendencies shaping the totality of power relations within a given social field during a particular period of time. From this perspective, 'cultural studies' might be best understood as a species of political sociology, with an analytical emphasis on the study of semiotic practices and a heavy bias towards qualitative modes of analysis. Its primary objective is to map power relations of all kinds in a given social field, with particular attention to the ways in which those relations are changing at a given moment.[21]

Such an analysis consequently aims at critically understanding the complexities of hegemonic formations as they are expressed in the political, social, economic and cultural fields. It is the comprehensive analysis of power formations as they play out in a historical moment, and therefore, they aim to understand hegemony in its particular temporality.

The current conjuncture, I contend, is pervaded by a sense of pessimism that is situated at a multitude of sites. As a dominant affect, it might not be endorsed in official ideologies, but it finds itself in the affective disposition of wide sections of the public in Western societies, in cultural texts such as literature, film and popular music, as well as in an ever-expanding body of intellectual work by philosophers and cultural theorists. I build on more recent approaches to pessimism which have re-connected it to its affective and emotional dimensions, most notably Sara Ahmed's notion of pessimism as an "alien affect".[22] Ahmed, as well as other theorists such as Lauren Berlant and Sianne Ngai, has developed wide-ranging accounts of negative affect which can be said to feed into the conjuncture's "organization of pessimism".[23] The sociologist Andreas Reckwitz has recently identified these negative affects as the negative image of the "positive culture of emotions" which characterise late neoliberal modernity in the West.[24] The "late-modern individual" is growing increasingly weary of the constant demand for positive "self-actualization".[25] The open promises of this entrepreneurial culture of self-actualisation which excludes "ugly feelings"[26] are increasingly being exposed as empty. Reckwitz's analysis points to a dialectics of the imperative of positive self-actualisation: The impasses of optimising, positive and hedonistic "self-transformation"[27] become ever more visible in the face of pervasive economic precarisation, and thus increasingly produce undesired negative emotions. This is a fundamental crisis of late-modern subject culture: the cultivation of one's best self feeds into the current cultural logic of the worst.[28]

In my take on pessimism as an affective as well as intellectual pattern I also draw on recent work by Eugene Thacker. His aphoristic writings on pessimism in *Cosmic Pessimism* and *Infinite Resignation* explore pessimist philosophical traditions (or rather their refusal to belong to any philosophical tradition) in both their philosophical seriousness and what one could call, following Paul de Man, pessimism's "resistance to theory",[29] and pessimism's status in "everyday life"[30] and as a melancholic disposition.[31] Considering the conjuncture as an "organization of pessimism" allows for exploring the different sites and vectors of contemporary pessimism in a more nuanced way.

A Haunted Conjuncture: Pessimism and Temporality

The loss of the future is a fundamentally hauntological concern. Since Jacques Derrida coined the concept in the early 1990s as a response to Francis Fukuyama's thesis of the post-communist "end of history", hauntology has been appropriated in the context of cultural, literary and media studies as a critical attempt at "presenting new ways of thinking about the past, present and future, rather than just the 'end' of history and of the twentieth century".[32] Hauntology is a way to utilise spectres and hauntings as figures that represent the paradoxical and destabilised experience of time and space.[33] For Mark Fisher, who popularised hauntology in the twenty-first century, "[t]he future is always experienced as a haunting: a virtuality that already impinges on the present, conditioning expectations and motivating cultural production".[34] Hauntological artworks and media engage with the haunting of the future in an act of mourning. For instance, hauntological electronic music mourns both the failure of the future to materialise "as actuality" and its disappearance of its "effective virtuality".[35] Hauntology, through the figure of the spectre, deconstructs the "fixity of the temporal" by confronting and infusing the present with "the possibility of alternative pasts and futures".[36] This is what hauntology and pessimism share. Pessimism, as a philosophy, is an intervention into dominant notions of temporality.[37]

Pessimism negates the notion of unchallenged continuous human progress and "attacks the roots of modern political orders by denying their sense of time".[38] Its negational stance is often considered unconstructive, counterproductive and obstructive. And yet, pessimism's reflections on time can be an ethical and even political project—it cannot, as Joshua Foa Dienstag has argued, be fully divorced from the notion of progress. Rather, both have emerged as specifically modern ideas. Pessimism is thus the "hidden twin" of progress.[39] In that, pessimism shares sensibilities with the concept of hauntology which considers the present to be disrupted by hauntings from the political and cultural past and potential futures. In hauntology the figure of the spectre becomes a vehicle to think of this temporal disjuncture.

Likewise, pessimism haunts contemporary culture as the spectral "doppelgänger" of progress and fundamentally unsettles linear temporalities. While it questions the dominant sense of time, pessimism's relationship to temporality goes even further in that it is itself always *untimely*. "No one has time for pessimism",[40] its complaining and disruptive voice always raised at an inopportune moment. Like untimely critique voiced in times of crisis, pessimism points to the "rupture of temporal continuity".[41] In its cosmic variant, it also invites views of futures in which humans will be merely ghosts, a spectral memory.

But pessimism goes one step further than hauntology in that it always confronts the present with the worst possible alternative future. It is not just that pessimism suggests that the future may be uncertain. It also asserts that whatever the future might bring, it will definitely be the worst possible one—"[f]or pessimism the world is brimming with negative possibility".[42] From a pessimist perspective, the future is already effective in the present, at least as a potentiality that is evoked in feelings towards the future as well as in modes of anticipation such as predictions, whether they are scientific, political, economic, religious or personal, and fears and desires for the future that shape the present.[43] This becomes even more problematic when considering the current crisis of the future. For Mark Fisher, hauntology was the expression of the loss of the future described by Franco Berardi and others—the lack of a utopian vision or even an alternative to the current state of affairs that Fisher called "capitalist realism".[44]

The current cultural logic of the worst is a continuation of this tendency. This, as Amy J. Elias has argued, also has a dramatic effect on the present. "We post-moderns", she observes, "have lost this sense of progress, but we also lose the present as it disappears not into the future, but into an uneasy mixture of pre- and post-Enlightenment thinking about the relation between past and future time".[45] Elias' description of the crisis of the tools of prognosis resonates with the anxious pessimism of Gen Z and Millennials in that it likewise renders humanity as being "dragged forward into a future that seems already in place".[46] Elias' assessment of the post-modern attitude towards temporality echoes both hauntological and pessimist concerns.

The future, then, is not only something that already takes effect in the present—through pre-emptive or anticipatory action. Rather, the future happens to us. A pessimist perspective is deeply suspicious of the ability to predict or anticipate the future in order to master time or humanity's existence in time. From a eudaemonic perspective, pessimist thought questions the possibility of happiness as the point of human life. However, pessimism can at least name the sources of human unhappiness, among which the "ontological misalignment between human beings and the world they inhabit"[47] is probably the most central one. In other words, pessimism establishes that the world is not there to please the human beings inhabiting it. Pessimism identifies the "ontological misalignment" in the anthropocentric misconception of a "world-for-us".[48] The notion of "ontological misalignment" is another aspect that pessimism shares with hauntology. Derrida coined the term as a phonetic play on the homophonous French words "ontologie" and "hantologie".[49] A hauntological perspective focuses on ontological ruptures in the human experience of history and temporality.

PESSIMIST ONTO-EPISTEMOLOGIES

Pessimism's "ontological misalignment" ultimately has epistemological repercussions. A pessimist epistemology can, for one, be akin to what Eva Horn describes as the "paradoxes of prediction": forecasting becomes a knowledge of the future as a "knowledge under the condition of not knowing", or awareness of the "known unknowns".[50] Its principle of futility, if brought to the final conclusion, is a radical corrective to the human perspective on the world and on being and knowledge. "Futility pervades pessimism", as Eugene Thacker observes, and failure becomes a "metaphysical principle"[51]: "Nothing you do makes a difference because everything you do makes a difference. [...]. By having a goal, planning ahead, and thinking things through carefully, we attempt, in a daily Prometheanism, to turn fatality to our advantage, to gain a glimpse of an order that seems buried deeper and deeper in the fabric of the universe."[52] For Thacker, (cosmic) pessimism is a matter of scale: if you do not see the downside of something, then this is simply because you do not yet have the adequate perspective to see the whole picture: "disorder is the order we don't yet see".[53] A cosmic pessimism in particular offers a "drastic scaling-up or scaling-down of the human point of view" that moves from an anthropocentric perspective to an "unhuman orientation of deep space and deep time".[54] As an epistemology, then, pessimist thought can generate a decentring of the individual, the subject and the human in time.

Pessimism offers opportunities for new prefigurative epistemologies in the face of an increasingly precarious futurity. This does not mean, however, that it is a more "realistic" outlook than any other, including optimism. Despite various claims that a pessimistic stance can in certain situations be a more "realistic" and therefore "useful" perspective to confront reality and its problems, whether they be personal, political or planetary, philosophers such as Eugene Thacker point out that being "realistic" and "realism", philosophically speaking, cannot be reduced to one handy definition. There might be situations in which pessimism is a "realistic" perspective—Thacker uses the example of depressive realism in which the pessimist has a much more realistic, that is, appropriate, assessment of their personal capability of control, does not fall victim to the optimism bias and "holds no illusions about their superiority over other people".[55] However, as Thacker points out, being realistic is mostly more a necessity than pessimism, which more often than not is a "luxury" in that it is not immediately useful in its focus on the worst.[56] This leads to the question of epistemology. As recent theorists of pessimism such as Eugene Thacker and R. Radhakrishnan have pointed out, a pessimist view is first and foremost just that: it is a *perspective* on a thing (an ontic thing), but it is not identical with the *actual quality* or characteristics of this thing. This is where the worn-out image of the glass half-empty comes in: The amount of water in the glass is empirically the same, no matter whether you describe its content as "half empty" or "half full". What matters here is the outlook, the perspective and the judgement resulting from this perspective. For Thacker, moral pessimism is marked by its view, no matter what the object of its view is:

> The moral pessimist at his or her height can take any phenomenon, no matter how apparently joyful, beneficial, or happy, and turn it into the worst possible scenario (even if only to note that every positive only paves the way for a negative). This is the typical view of the glass being half-empty. Note that moral pessimism is pessimistic because its view is pessimistic, irrespective of what is happening in the world.[57]

This view is no more realistic than its opposite, an optimistic perspective. Consequently, R. Radhakrishnan has asked the necessary question about the epistemological value of pessimism: "If pessimism is a world-view and not just a deviant or abnormal or eccentric perspective on reality, then surely, it should be allowed to stand on its own epistemological grounds."[58]

Radhakrishnan chooses the example of afropessimism to illustrate his point. Afropessimism is a relatively recent line of theorising which re-reads and continues earlier strands of Black radical thought, such as Frantz Fanon, James Baldwin and others (which does not mean that these authors would have necessarily subscribed to these readings of their works, had they had the opportunity for comment).[59] The afropessimist thesis is in short: the history of slavery in the US is the foundation of the condition of white versus Black subjectivity and ontological status. Slavery has constructed Black being as the very antithesis of the human. The idea of the human thus does not include Black subjects; it has established white people as the very essence of the human.[60] For Radhakrishnan, afropessimism as a perspective is a matter of choice:

> Afro-Pessimism's quarrel [] is not just historical, but historiographic and meta-historical. Unless and until the very history of current history is destroyed and a new history re-invented *ex nihilo*, Afro-Pessimism's response is a No in thunder. The point I want to make is that Afro-Pessimism could see this in a different manner, cognitively speaking; but it *wills* not to. [...]. It is by way of a supreme act of will that Afro-Pessimism chooses to be pessimistic.[61]

Afropessimism, then—and this holds equally true for most other pessimisms—moves from epistemology (knowing the world in a certain way) to ontology (the being of Black bodies) and, finally, to temporality (knowing the being of Black bodies in history). It thus offers a rigorous perspective through which to know the status and function of Black life and being (primarily) in the post-slavery USA. Radhakrishnan's argument about afropessimism's epistemology is echoed in Wilderson's book *Afropessimism*, a blend of theory and autobiography in which Wilderson details his journey of becoming an Afropessimist. Wilderson starts by stating that he "was no Afropessimist in 1988" and merely "saw myself as a degraded Human, saw my plight as analogous to the Palestinians, the Native American, and the working class".[62] But by gradually shifting his perspective on his own experience of oppression, he realises that he "was the foil of Humanity. Humanity looked to me when it was unsure of itself. I let Humanity say, with a sigh of existential relief, 'At least we're not him'."[63] In other words, Wilderson comes to identify with a particular epistemology of Black lives which leads him to an ontological theory of Black being as the opposite of "Human", rooted in the history of slavery. Thus, to come back to Radhakrishnan, Wilderson chooses to see the temporality of Black being in a particular way that Gloria Wekker in a critical review of his book has called a "metatheory" about the "Black/Slave" as "ontologically absent, a living dead person".[64] It should be pointed out here that Wekker rejects Wilderson's theses precisely on the grounds of his historically exclusive, selective and essentialist approach to African American identity and confesses that she finds it "shocking [that] many, especially of the younger generation [...] apparently find [Afropessimism] so attractive".[65] Wilderson's book strikes her as "loveless, hopeless and divisive"[66] which, ironically, is probably what most pessimist theories set out to be to some degree. The example of afropessimism thus demonstrates the relationship of temporality, epistemology and ontology in pessimist thinking.

What is more, afropessimism points to a blurring of ontological and epistemological preoccupations, which is characteristic of many of the contemporary new pessimisms. Identity-focussed pessimisms such as afropessimism and queer pessimism speak to the profoundly uncertain onto-epistemic status of being in the world and knowing other being in the world. The same can be said of eco-pessimistic approaches such as Timothy Morton's dark ecology and Patricia MacCormack's ahumanism. For MacCormack, ahumanism entails the radical rethinking of the human obsession with identity in favour of a "queering" of the human species in its relationship with the world and "with our future": "Disengaging from rigid systems of signification and subjectification enters us into a queer relation with the world because all we can do is ask questions. How do we listen to the world? How can we hear in languages and through expressions which affect us very differently to human significations?"[67] MacCormack's conception of queering the human challenges what she identifies as a "self-absorption" of both "minoritarian" and "majoritarian" identities, which are both part of the "foundation of anthropocentric hubris".[68] She envisions a "queering" of the human as anticipating a future that decentres the human and its micro-forms: "It is time for humans to stop being human".[69]

While MacCormack is at pains to stress that she by no means wants to diminish the struggle of "minoritarians" against various kinds of oppression, her radical statements must nonetheless be considered a provocation in times when some groups, to paraphrase the afropessimist argument, argue that they even struggle to be included in the human in the first place. MacCormack, however, argues that the very basis for struggles over identities and subjectivities "comes from power—the power to name [...] once again, like the nonhuman, we are struggling with an epistemic system which we did not create and within which we can claim no benefit".[70] In other words, then, "minoritarian" identity struggles for recognition are really just perpetuating categories of knowing human groups and individuals within the pre-given frames that caused oppression and disadvantage in the first place. MacCormack's intervention can thus be read as the extreme onto-epistemological endpoint to current developments in pessimism in that it, on the one hand, rejects what she polemically calls the universalist pessimism of the "white male wail"[71] and, on the other, exposes the epistemological and political impasses of current identity discourses. Thus, as Packer and Stoneman argue, MacCormack's Deleuzeo-Guattarian approach explores "pessimism's deterritorializing potentiality as a means of charting an emancipatory reterritorialization, rather than achieving the absolute deterritorialization of Schopenhauerian pessimism".[72]

As the discussion of "new" pessimisms has demonstrated thus far, ontological, epistemological and temporal aspects are being fought over in what could be considered a struggle over the "right" kind of pessimism that identifies the "right" kind of worst. This is a struggle that is being fought as much in scholarly discourse as it is expressed in the areas of culture. It will be one of the main aims of this present book to put these different pessimisms in dialogue with each other, to identify the similarities, shared aims as well as differences and points of conflict. To illustrate how these different aspects play out, I will now turn to a recent literary text, Hari Kunzru's novel *Red Pill* (2020). Kunzru's text is particularly illustrative since it deals with representative cultural and political moments which mark the current conjuncture. Set in the year 2016 in the runup to the American presidential election that marked the beginning of Donald Trump's time in office, with the 2015/2016 refugee crisis and the rise of the alt-right as the backdrop, the novel dissects the ontological, epistemological and affective facets of pessimism, its conflicting political expressions and (ab)uses. It is a novel of ideas characterised by its narrator's apocalyptic sensibilities and is thus a paradigmatic text of the cultural logic of the worst—a prism with which the ideas for the present book can be outlined.

A Conjunctural Pessimist Text: Hari Kunzru's *Red Pill*

The narrator of Hari Kunzru's novel *Red Pill*, a Brooklyn-based writer of British-Indian heritage, is haunted by an unshakable sense of impending doom. At night, he obsesses about middle age, watches news reports about refugees, fears for the safety of his wife and daughter and worries about the ongoing election campaign of presidential candidate Donald Trump. What if he cannot protect his family should worse comes to worst? A fellowship at the ominous Deuter Center at Berlin Wannsee does not bring about the desired change of mind. Rather than focusing on his research on poetry, he morbidly sympathises with the suicidal poet Heinrich von Kleist, and instead of socialising with the other fellows, including the pompous neurophilosopher Edgar who scoffs at ideas of self, personhood and diversity-obsessed liberals, he hides in his room and binge-watches *Blue Lives*, an American police show whose title already hints at the right-wing counter slogan to the Black Lives Matter movement, "Blue Lives Matter", and whose cynical attitude towards human dignity and crude use of philosophical quotes by the likes of E. M. Cioran, Arthur Schopenhauer and Thomas Hobbes compels and appalls him in equal measure. It seems that the fictional show's maelstrom of nihilism and cruelty epitomises the unnamed narrator's worst fears about the future. *Blue Lives* conveys to him the "world's hopelessness",[73] its "very pessimistic tone"[74] a manifestation of his own fears of a future that "was unimaginably bleak and terrible".[75] At the same time, the show poses an onto-epistemological irritation for the narrator. Something seems off about the way the characters mouth their philosophical statements, thus disrupting the genre conventions of the fictional crime show spectacle. The narrator feels that the characters are addressing him, implicating him as being complicit with the show's transgressions by watching it.[76] It is as if the pessimistic philosophies espoused by the characters transcend the barrier between televised fiction and reality, touching the viewer. However, considering the increasingly mentally unstable and potentially unreliable narrator, who at times does not know whether he is being surveilled at the Deuter Center, this destabilisation of epistemological boundaries is likewise experienced by the readers of Kunzru's novel.

Kunzru's nameless protagonist—a thinly disguised fictionalisation of the author—is representative of the current cultural logic of the worst. He can imagine his own and humanity's future merely "as catastrophe".[77] For him, social, political and environmental collapse are imminent; the values that he and those close to him hold dear are under constant threat; his paranoid tendencies are exacerbated by his stay at the Deuter Center where it seems that he is under constant surveillance by staff and other fellows, his aesthetic, moral, political and spiritual principles continuously scrutinised in an atmosphere pregnant with the ghosts of Germany's past, the totalitarianism of Nazism and the German Democratic Republic. Kunzru's novel points to a crucial historical event that sets the stage for theories of hauntology: the fall of the Berlin Wall which, in Francis Fukuyama's terms, marked the "end of history"—a thesis which urged

Derrida to grapple with the deconstructive practice of hauntology.[78] Kunzru's protagonist is haunted by precisely this end of history, while he himself must realise that he fears the future and might be left behind (at best) or crushed (at worst) by the future course of history. He thus experiences the hauntological "temporality of the return".[79] What makes his hauntological experience a deeply pessimist one is the sense of history as a series of repetitions of cruelties, an anti-Enlightenment, catastrophic forward-movement. He feels his relatively privileged way of life to be under imminent threat by the emergence of Trump as a political candidate and what his presidency "means for people like us, the unreal Americans, the ones who the new president and his supporters hate most of all".[80] But it is not Trump alone who is responsible for the narrator's anxieties. Rather, he is a symptom—like the refugee crisis which he monitors closely, first from the safety of his computer, and then first-hand in his encounters with two refugees in the wintry streets of Berlin.

But despite his own pessimism, which seems to gradually tip into a state of paranoia and suspected psychosis, the troubled writer reacts with shock to any elevation of a pessimist outlook into a substantial worldview. The crime show *Blue Lives* intrigues and disgusts him precisely because it seems to affirm his worst worries about the human condition. When he meets the show's creator, Anton, he confronts him about the series' bleak subtext: "So that's it? Is that what you believe? That it's a war against each. That we're in hell?"[81] *Blue Lives* takes the narrator's own worries about the future to an extreme conclusion: a fundamentally misanthropic worldview according to which only those are prepared for the worst who are willing to rid themselves of any cosy humanist ideals and to accept the Hobbesian condition of a war against everyone.

Kunzru's novel thus confronts its protagonist with two kinds of dealing with the worst. In being confronted with Anton's bleak vision, the narrator realises that he is too weak to confront the worst of the world as he sees it. His pessimism is an ethical pessimism about the state of the world and the future, informed by his exploration of different pasts: the subject of his scholarly work, Heinrich von Kleist, the past of German fascism and his encounters with the witnesses of the Stasi totalitarianism of communist Eastern Germany. He is not only worried about his own and his family's well-being and the precariousness of life. He fears that the ethical, aesthetic and political values he holds dear will count for nothing should his fears turn out to be justified. Anton's vision embodies this loss of values, and, even more worryingly, in a disturbing twist Anton turns out to be

part of an international network of alt-right white supremacists. His celebration of white police officers in *Blue Lives* thus becomes the cultural
form underwriting the nihilism that paves the way for Trump. This is the
second kind of pessimism the novel's narrator is confronted with: a politi-
cised celebration of humanity's worst.

Both kinds of pessimism in *Red Pill* are symptomatic of what Lawrence
Grossberg has identified as the "organization of pessimism" prevalent
since the 2010s—a conjuncture characterised by "pessimism, cynicism,
apathy, bad moods".[82] Kunzru's novel navigates this "affective topography"[83] in which "[t]he future is no longer a promise but a threat, the 'end
of the world as we know it'".[84] *Red Pill* thus reflects the fundamental
ambiguity of pessimism. Derided as the "symptom of a bad attitude"[85] at
best and a pathological condition[86] or a regressive and reactionary political
attitude at worst,[87] pessimism is rarely a proud self-description and often
an accusation. And yet, pessimism cannot be pinned down exclusively to
one political or ideological position. Oswald Spengler's *Decline of the West*
(1918/1922) and his reactionary critique of parliamentary democracy or
Roger Scruton's conservative defence of *The Uses of Pessimism* (2010) as a
"realistic" outlook on politics bear the label as much as the negative dialectics of the Frankfurt School of Critical Theory. Politically speaking, pessimism is hard to pin down. This is reflected in Kunzru's novel when the
narrator asks Anton why he used a quote from the writings of Joseph de
Maistre in his show in an edited version which left out the "hope of salvation from the earthly meat grinder"—leaving the "meat grinder [...] all
there is".[88]

The writer, who is desperate for his world to regain some sort of stabil-
ity and fundament, finds Anton's cynical vision of the world as a mere
meat grinder, appalling precisely because he is struggling in his own work
and life to maintain a humanist vision. In Berlin, however, everyone seems
to be out to challenge and undermine his ideals. Anton mocks him as a
"believer in progress, religion of the liberals".[89] Anton's "nihilistic TV
show", in turn, makes "a mockery of human dignity",[90] and the obnox-
ious neurophilosopher Edgar, who represents positions reminiscent of the
German philosopher Thomas Metzinger's challenges to "the myth of the
self"[91] and of the nihilist philosopher Ray Brassier,[92] ridicules him for
believing in subjectivity, the self and the value of aesthetics. An Eastern-
German woman, who confesses to him her past as a Stasi informant and
subsequent excommunication from a group of radical punks and her exile
from German society, leaves him in disillusionment and criticises him for

his naïve faith in the good of humanity. What is at stake for the narrator is his idea of hope, purpose and humanist idealism. "You don't want something to hope for?",[93] he asks Anton, who rejects such whimsical sentiments. The pessimism the narrator is confronted with not only forces him to address his own anxiety about the future but also compels him to challenge his own principles. His well-intentioned attempts at rebuking Anton's dark worldview, however, are as pathetic as his desperate attempt to help out a homeless refugee and his daughter—actions which are being misread as the attempt of a paedophile to take advantage of the vulnerable child and which lead to a temporary arrest. Like his own daughter at home in New York, the threatened fictional children of the police officer protagonist in *Blue Lives* and the dead real-life child refugees the narrator sees in his newsfeed seemingly every day, the refugee girl he fails to help is an image of the precarious futurity that the narrator has become overwhelmed by.

It seems, then, that Anton's bleak vision of the world comes true for the narrator. The narrator is gradually convinced that the TV show creator is instrumental in an international alt-right plot (and maybe he is). Anton and his ideas haunt him—just like Anton predicted: "You know what the best part is? I'm going to be living rent free in your head from now on. You're going to think about me all the fucking time."[94] And indeed, the narrator's state deteriorates; he fills notebooks with his forays into cosmic pessimism, about humanity's "monkey bodies" in "a race against time".[95] It is here that Kunzru's novel fully realises the notion of a spectral pessimism that haunts and gradually pervades affect and thinking. The narrator's deep dive into pessimism begins as an act of liberal humanist resistance against the cynical, misanthropic ideas of a white supremacist, transitions into mental collapse, and ends on election day 6 November 2016, when the narrator, his wife and friends who supported the Hilary Clinton campaign are faced with the election victory of Donald Trump. For the narrator, who experiences "temporal disjuncture" in the hauntological sense, a perception of time as being out of joint, with a threatening future emerging spectrally in the present,[96] his pessimism becomes uncannily validated:

> up until now there have been two tracks of timelines: the one that Rei and this little group of our friends live on, in which the future is predictable, an extrapolation from the past, a steady progression in which we are gradually turning into our own mothers and fathers [...]. Then there's the second track, the occult track on which all this normality is a paper screen over

something bloody and atavistic that is rising up out of history to meet us. I am the ragged membrane, the porous barrier between the two. [...]. My madness, the madness for which I've been medicated and therapized and involuntarily detained, is about to become everyone's madness.[97]

In other words, his hauntological experience of not quite being in the here and now of his fellow human beings, and his pessimism as affect merge as the current conjuncture reveals its true political and ideological structure. It is here that the different notions of pessimism that characterise the current cultural moment merge: pessimism as personal disposition, pessimism as integral to the "affective topography" of the conjuncture. The narrator's experience of two different timelines, which is also a difference in affective subjectivities, reflects the late-modern experience of precarious temporality and its failure of prognosis.[98] It is now no longer possible to draw a reliable "horizon of expectation" out of the past "space of experience".[99] Quite fittingly, this collapse of progressive futurity is brought on by the rise of Donald Trump, whose reactionary and "retrotopian"[100] slogan "Make America Great Again" promises to restore a national narrative of the past and is thus symptomatic of the loss of futurity. The only thing that is possible and thinkable "after the future"[101] is "retrofuture".[102]

The struggle for the mastery of temporality and futurity at the heart of *Red Pill* make Kunzru's novel the paradigmatic narrative representation of the current conjuncture's "organization of pessimism". It depicts the intersections of pessimism as affect and pessimism as onto-epistemological assessment of the world as well as the different and conflicting political registers within which this assessment may take shape. This struggle over the future is, ultimately, a struggle over "reality" or, more precisely, humans' claim to "reality". While in the end the narrator is still not certain whether he has "filled [his] brain with obsolete philosophies" or whether his "intuitions about reality are likely false", he concludes that Anton's neo-Hobbesian alt-right nihilo-pessimism is equally limited in its truth claims, and that "[w]hat Anton and his capering friends in their red hats call realism—the truth that they think they understand—is just the cynical operation of power".[103] The narrator identifies this type of pessimism, which sees human beings in perpetual conflict with each other if left to their own devices, as a way of keeping people in fear of each other. There is, indeed, a hint at "radical utopianism"[104] in the narrator's final lines: "That's how they want us. Isolated. Prey."[105] But the conclusion is not to succumb to perpetual conflict but to resist hostility: "So we must find each other. We must remember that we do not exist alone."[106] This, however, is not a retreat into facile optimism. It is, rather, an optimism of the will born from a pessimism of the intellect—an acknowledgement of the worst, but also an affirmation of possibilities of resistance which open up the horizon of expectations and create a new futurity: "Outside the wide world is howling and scratching at the window. Tomorrow we will have no choice but to let it in."[107]

Spectres of Pessimism

Kunzru's novel interrogates the precarious temporalities of the current conjuncture and points to its multiple trajectories of futurity. The narrator's experience of different timelines which run parallel to each other and occasionally clash or intersect demonstrates the different horizons of expectation shaped by contingent political and cultural worldviews, from the anxiety about a catastrophic future to the hope (or "cruel optimism"[108]) for a progressive future and the retrotopian ideal of a backwards-looking future. These conflicting futurities manifest themselves, in Mark Fisher's terms, as hauntings in the present. Likewise, pessimism, as an affect and a philosophy, becomes part of these hauntings. The spectres of pessimism pervade the present in the form of virtual manifestations of uncertain futures. As becomes apparent in the conflicting horizons of expectations, however, this pessimism is also always in tension with utopian potentialities. As John Storey has pointed out, the retrotopian and dystopian visions of the political present compel others to oppose them and find utopian hope in such dystopian conditions.[109] Likewise, Patricia MacCormack might argue that her vision of an ahuman future is not so much a pessimist one (even though it is undoubtedly a misanthropic one), but a hopeful utopian one.

The present book will address these tensions between pessimism and utopianism by exploring past and present theories and cultural texts. Chapter 2, "From Pessimism of Theory to Radical Utopianism: Gramsci, Critical Theory and Cultural Studies", retraces the dialectic of the pessimism of the intellect and the optimism of the will from its use in the thought of Antonio Gramsci, its appropriation in Stuart Hall's practice of cultural studies and conjunctural analysis, and compares it with Theodor Adorno and Max Horkheimer's similar idea of a pessimism of theory and a pessimism of practice. This comparison of Frankfurt School Critical Theory and Birmingham Cultural Studies extrapolates their shared utopian and pessimist ideas and thus proposes a cultural theory of pessimism that can be used to make sense of the current conjuncture and the notion of melancholic hope that can be found in recent works by John Storey, Shona Hunter and Mathias Thaler. The dialectic of utopianism and pessimism is further discussed in Chap. 3, "Undoing Better Worlds: Anti-Utopianism from Cioran to Afropessimism". The chapter expands on the notion of progress and the role of utopia in politics, philosophy, cultural theory and arts. Through a reading of E. M. Cioran's critique of utopianism and a comparison with John Storey's more recent theorisations of utopianism as well as in afrofuturism and afropessimism, the chapter discusses artistic and (sub)cultural explorations of utopianism and pessimism.

Chapter 4, "The Kids Will Not Be Alright: Grievable Futures and the Ethics of Reproductive Pessimism", turns to recent debates on the ethics of human reproduction in the antinatalist philosophy of David Benatar and in Lee Edelman and Sara Ahmed's queer pessimism. Antinatalism is expressive of a strand of recent new pessimisms and has gained traction and garnered controversy. The tenet that humans should stop reproducing to prevent the suffering of ever more sentient beings and to minimise humanity's damaging impact on other life forms is one of the most radical practical conclusions of pessimist thought. Its ideas also offer opportunities for thought experiments with temporality and futurity. What will a future without humans look like? Can we mourn the future? What temporal implications does Benatar's "better to never have been" offer? Such thought experiments tie in with narrative experiments in film and literature. The chapter analyses the ethics of procreation in Gaspar Noé's film *Irréversible* (2002), Ted Chiang's short story "Story of Your Life" (1998/2002) and its film adaptation, Denis Villeneuve's *Arrival* (2016). These texts experiment with narrative time and the question of what a potential knowability of the future would mean for the ethics of procreation.

Building on the previous chapter's conclusions about pessimist futurity and antinatalist philosophy, Chap. 5, "Embracing the Apocalypse: Extinction, Cosmic Pessimism and Ahuman Futures", addresses the future as the end. It considers philosophies of antinatalism, ahumanism and extinctionism in the works of Ray Brassier, Patricia MacCormack, David Benatar, Eugene Thacker and Thomas Ligotti. The "end as affirmation"[110] has also found expression in fiction and film. The chapter traces pessimist philosophies in apocalyptic narratives in Lars von Trier's film *Melancholia* (2011), Camille Griffin's film *Silent Night* (2021) and Thomas Ligotti's short story "The Nightmare Network" (2002). These narratives offer a poetics of extinction that makes them radically cosmic-pessimist texts.

The conclusion reflects on the insights that the analyses of the philosophical, political and cultural texts in this book have provided and argues for pessimism as a mode of affective and ideological disruption that can critically interrogate narratives of progress from a variety of angles. Pessimism will continue to haunt culture in times of overly optimistic hopes for solutions to the social, political and ecological problems of the present and future such as "sustainable growth", techno fix solutions or the belief that continuous growth or acceleration will be a fix to the ailments of the capitalocene.

The conclusion "Cultural Studies, Prefigurative Thought and the (Ab) Uses of Pessimism" will challenge such hopes and point out how pessimism, as a disruptive mode, can intervene into such debates. Thus, this chapter will challenge the prevalent idea that pessimism is equivalent with a passive giving in to the worst that undermines political agency. It will be argued that contrary to general opinion, optimism can lead to political inactivity when it is merely expressed in a passive, hopeful projection of improvement into the future. By taking up the notions of the "end as affirmation" and as something that has already happened (heeding Timothy Morton's call for a "philosophy after the end of the world"[111]) as well as of the dictum of "pessimism of the intellect, optimism of the will", this conclusion points out the benefits of a pessimist mode of cultural analysis.

NOTES

1. "The Deloitte Global Millennial and GenZ Survey 2021", p. 26.
2. "Deloitte 2021", p. 15.
3. Berardi, Franco "Bifo", *After the Future* (Edinburgh: AK Press, 2011), p. 23.
4. Lawrence Grossberg, *Cultural Studies in the Future Tense* (Durham: Duke University Press, 2010), p. 40.
5. Amy J. Elias, "Past/Future", in *Time: A Vocabulary of the Present* (New York: New York University Press, 2016), 35–50, p. 44.
6. Lawrence Grossberg und Bryan G. Behrenshausen, "Cultural Studies and Deleuze-Guattari, Part 2: From Affect to Conjunctures", *Cultural Studies* 30, No. 6 (1. November 2016): 1001–1028, p. 1025.
7. Eugene Thacker, *Cosmic Pessimism* (Minneapolis: Univocal, 2015a), p. 3.
8. Joseph Packer and Ethan Stoneman, *A Feeling of Wrongness* (University Park: Penn State University Press, 2018), p. 17.

9. Patricia MacCormack, *The Ahuman Manifesto: Activism for the End of the Anthropocene* (London: Bloomsbury, 2020), p. 153–154. Ironically, David Benatar, in contrast to Patricia MacCormack, associates notions of masculinity with optimism rather than pessimism. He accuses optimists who condemn pessimism of a "smug macho tone" in their dismissal of the "perceived weakness of the pessimist", David Benatar, *Better Never to Have Been: The Harm of Coming Into Existence* (Oxford: Oxford University Press, 2006), pp. 210–211).

10. Packer/Stoneman 2018, p. 18.

11. Eugene Thacker, *In the Dust of This Planet: Horror of Philosophy Vol. 1* (Winchester: Zero Books, 2011), p. 5.

12. For an account of Lovecraft's pessimist and misanthropic poetics, see Michel Houellebecq, *H.P. Lovecraft: Against the World, Against Life* (London: Gollansz, 2008).

13. Packer/Stoneman, 2018, pp. 49–78.

14. Sara Ahmed, *The Promise of Happiness* (Durham: Duke University Press, 2010), p. 162.

15. Ahmed, 2010, p. 162.

16. Joe Bailey, *Pessimism* (London: Routledge, 1988); Oliver Bennett, *Cultural Pessimism: Narratives of Decline in the Postmodern World* (Edinburgh: Edinburgh University Press, 2001).

17. Joshua Foa Dienstag, *Pessimism: Philosophy, Ethic, Spirit* (New Jersey: Princeton University Press, 2006), p. 6, footnote 3. Williams' concept has also been criticised within cultural studies. See, for example, Stuart Hall: *Cultural Studies 1983* (Durham: Duke University Press, 2017), pp. 50–51.

18. Dienstag, 2006, p. 4.

19. Dienstag, 2006, p. 45.

20. Grossberg, 2010, pp. 40–41.

21. Jeremy Gilbert, 'This Conjuncture: For Stuart Hall', *New Formations* 96, no. 96 (26 July 2019): 5–37, p. 6.

22. Ahmed, 2010, p. 162.

23. Grossberg/Behrenshausen, 2016, p. 1022. See also Sianne Ngai, *Ugly Feelings* (Cambridge, Mass: Harvard University Press, 2007) and Lauren Berlant, *Cruel Optimism* (Durham: Duke University Press, 2011).

24. Andreas Reckwitz, *The End of Illusions: Politics, Economy and Culture in Late Modernity* (Cambridge: Polity Press, 2021), p. 112.

25. Reckwitz, 2021, p. 110.

26. Ngai, 2007.

27. Reckwitz, 2021, p. 110.

28. I use the term "cultural logic of the worst" in reference to Eugene Thacker's explanation of philosophical pessimism's "logics of the worst"

as being "structured around two qualitative statements"—one about metaphysics, "which makes a claim about the world, life, or even being as such", and the other about humanism and human subjectivity's grasp on the world, life and the self (Eugene Thacker, *Starry Speculative Corpse: Horror of Philosophy 2* (Winchester: Zero Books, 2015b), pp. 143–144.

29. Paul de Man, *The Resistance to Theory* (Minneapolis: University of Minnesota Press, 2006), pp. 3–20.
30. Eugene Thacker, *Infinite Resignation* (London: Repeater, 2018), p. 6.
31. Thacker, 2018, p. 11.
32. Katy Shaw, *Hauntology: The Presence of the Past in Twenty-First Century English Literature.* (Houndsmills: Palgrave, 2018), p. 5.
33. Shaw, 2018, p. 2.
34. Mark Fisher, "What Is Hauntology?", *Film Quarterly* 66, Nr. 1 (2012): 16–24, p. 16.
35. Fisher, 2012, p. 16.
36. Shaw, 2018, p. 7.
37. Dienstag, 2006, pp. 19–36.
38. Dienstag, 2006, p. 5.
39. Dienstag, 2006, p. 16.
40. Thacker, 2015a, p. 4.
41. Wendy Brown, *Edgework. Critical Essays on Knowledge and Politics* (New Jersey: Princeton University Press, 2009), p. 7.
42. Thacker, 2015a, p. 9.
43. Bailey, 1988, p. 2.
44. Mark Fisher, *Capitalist Realism. Is There No Alternative?* (Winchester: Zero Books, 2009).
45. Elias, 2016, p. 44.
46. Elias, 2016, p. 44.
47. Dienstag, 2006, p. 33.
48. Thacker, 2015a, p. 12.
49. Jacques Derrida, *Specters of Marx: The State of the Debt, the Work of Mourning and the New International* (Abingdon: Routledge, 2011), p. 63.
50. Eva Horn, *The Future as Catastrophe* (New York: Columbia University Press, 2018), p. 177.
51. Thacker, 2015a, p. 14.
52. Thacker, 2015a, pp. 14–15.
53. Thacker, 2015a, p. 15.
54. Thacker, 2015a, p. 13.
55. Thacker, 2015b, p. 157.
56. Thacker, 2015b, p. 157.
57. Thacker, 2015b, p. 138.

58. R. Radhakrishan, "The Epistemology of Pessimism", *The Comparatist* 43 (2019): 41–67, p. 42
59. Frank B. Wilderson III draws on Frantz Fanon and James Baldwin throughout his book *Afropessimism* (New York: Liferight, 2021).
60. See for instance Wilderson III., 2021 and Jared Sexton, "The Social Life of Social Death: On Afro-Pessimism and Black Optimism." Anna M. Agathangelou und Kyle D. Killian, eds., *Time, Temporality and Violence in International Relations: (De)fatalizing the Present, Forging Radical Alternatives*, (Abingdon: Routledge, 2016).
61. Radhakrishnan, 2019, p. 48.
62. Wilderson III., 2021, p. 13.
63. Wilderson III., 2021, p. 13.
64. Gloria Wekker, "Afropessimism", *European Journal of Women's Studies* 28, no. 1 (1 February 2021): 86–97, p. 89.
65. Wekker, 2021, p. 90.
66. Wekker, 2021, p. 86.
67. MacCormack, 2020, pp. 63–64.
68. MacCormack, 2020, p. 39.
69. MacCormack, 2020, p. 65.
70. MacCormack, 2020, p. 58.
71. Qtd. in Packer/Stoneman, 2018, p. 18.
72. Packer/Stoneman, 2018, p. 18.
73. Hari Kunzru, *Red Pill.* (London: Simon & Schuster, 2021), p. 84.
74. Kunzru, 2021, p. 163.
75. Kunzru, 2021, pp. 75–76.
76. Kunzru, 2021, pp. 72–73.
77. Horn, 2018.
78. Shaw, 2018, p. 5.
79. Shaw, 2018, p. 6.
80. Kunzru, 2021, p. 281.
81. Kunzru, 2021, p. 163.
82. Grossberg/Behrenshausen, 2016, p. 1022.
83. Grossberg/Behrenshausen, 2016, p. 1022.
84. Horn, 2018, p. 174.
85. Thacker, 2015a, p. 3.
86. Cf. Bennett, 2001, p. 183.
87. For a discussion of political and cultural pessimism and a discussion of Oswald Spengler in particular, see Jan-Paul Klünder, *Politischer Pessimismus: Negative Weltkonstruktion und politische Handlungs(un)möglichkeit bei Carl Schmitt, Michel Foucault und Giorgio Agamben* (Bielefeld: Transcript, 2017), pp. 9–10.
88. Kunzru, 2021, p. 165.

89. Kunzru, 2021, p. 165.
90. Kunzru, 2021, p. 166.
91. Thomas Metzinger, *The Ego Tunnel: The Science of the Mind and the Myth of the Self* (New York: BasicBooks, 2009).
92. Ray Brassier, *Nihil Unbound: Enlightenment and Extinction* (Houndsmills: Palgrave, 2007).
93. Kunzru, 2021, p. 165.
94. Kunzru, 2021, p. 185.
95. Kunzru, 2021, p. 228.
96. Shaw, 2018, p. 9.
97. Kunzru, 2021, p. 280.
98. Elias, 2016, p. 38.
99. Elias, 2016, pp. 36–38; Reinhart Koselleck, *Futures Past. On the Semantics of Historical Time* (New York: Columbia University Press, 2004).
100. Zygmunt Bauman, *Retrotopia* (Cambridge: Polity Press, 2017); see also John Storey, *Radical Utopianism and Cultural Studies: On Refusing to Be Realistic* (London: Routledge, 2019), p. 109.
101. Berardi, 2011.
102. Elias, 2016, p. 40
103. Kunzru, 2021, p. 283.
104. Storey, 2019.
105. Kunzru, 2021, p. 282.
106. Kunzru, 2021, p. 282.
107. Kunzru, 2021, p. 283.
108. Berlant, 2011.
109. Storey, 2019, p. 113.
110. MacCormack, 2020, p. 1.
111. Timothy Morton, *Hyperobjects: Philosophy and Ecology after the End of the World*, (Minneapolis: University of Minnesota Press, 2013).

CHAPTER 2

From Pessimism of Theory to Radical Utopianism: Gramsci, Critical Theory and Cultural Studies

Abstract This chapter provides a comparative analysis of pessimism in the political thought of the Marxist Antonio Gramsci, of the Critical Theory of Max Horkheimer and Theodor Adorno and of cultural studies theorist Stuart Hall. Gramsci, Critical Theory and Hall's cultural studies share variations of the phrase "pessimism of the intellect, optimism of the will"— a dictum that Gramsci uses throughout his *Prison Notebooks*. It captures the dialectic relationship of a rigorous analysis of a historical conjuncture with political practice. Gramsci's approach also informs Hall's appropriation of conjunctural analysis in the context of cultural studies. The chapter historically traces the dialectic of analytical pessimism and utopian optimism in these bodies of work and identifies it as a central component for a conjunctural analysis of the cultural, political and affective aspects of the contemporary cultural logic of the worst, that is, the subject of this book. The chapter concludes with a reflection on the place of pessimist analysis and hopeful utopian thought in contemporary cultural theorising vis-à-vis more radical strands of contemporary pessimism.

Keywords Critical Theory • Cultural Studies • Pessimism of the intellect/optimism of the will • Utopianism • Antonio Gramsci • Theodor Adorno • Max Horkheimer • Stuart Hall

© The Author(s), under exclusive license to Springer Nature
Switzerland AG 2023
M. Schmitt, *Spectres of Pessimism*,
https://doi.org/10.1007/978-3-031-25351-5_2

POLITICAL PESSIMISM

After 1945, new strands of social and cultural theory developed in Western academia. With the emergence of new media technologies and the diversification of what would be known as "popular culture", and with the social, political and ideological reorientations of the post-war age, new explanatory models came to the fore to speak to the changing times. In Germany, the theorists of the Frankfurt School took up the challenge to continue a version of Marxist thinking that was able to adapt to the political realities of post-fascist Western capitalism on the one hand and the authoritarian distortion of socialism and Marxism in the Soviet Union on the other. Formed during the time of the Weimar Republic, the Frankfurt Institute for Social Research—with many of its members coming from Jewish families and rooted in Marxist thought—was forced to emigrate from Germany once the Nazis took power and started to systematically attack intellectual institutions. During their time in the US, Max Horkheimer and Theodor Adorno continued the project of Critical Theory. While for Horkheimer and Adorno Critical Theory was a way to come to terms with German fascism, its causes and paradoxes, their experience with American culture was equally informative. Their collaborative work culminated in the *Dialectic of Enlightenment* (1944).[1] The book offers a complex theorisation of fascism and antisemitism that not only addresses the question of how the atrocities and barbarism of two World Wars and the Holocaust were possible in the post-Enlightenment age but also considered American mass culture as a system that was instrumental in the wider "mass deception" of Western capitalism and therefore complicit with, if not instrumental to, fascism.

In Britain, the newly emerging field of cultural studies was less pessimistic about the social and cultural shifts in post-war society. The theoretical and methodological orientation of the Birmingham Centre for Contemporary Cultural Studies (CCCS) founded by Richard Hoggart and Stuart Hall in 1964 was rooted in Raymond Williams' insistence on culture as the "relationships between elements in a whole way of life"[2] and Hall's Gramscian approach to culture as the arena in which the wars of position over hegemony were being fought attested popular culture the potential to not only deceive the masses but also to be a means of subversion. So, would it be accurate to reduce the Frankfurt School to the pessimists and the Birmingham School to the optimists amongst the post-Marxist cultural theorists? Only to a certain extent. While it is true that, as John Storey has argued, the Birmingham School of cultural studies rejects the "pessimistic elitism"[3] with which Adorno and Horkheimer dissect popular culture, and indeed sees the popular as a site of struggle over meaning and cultural hegemony, Stuart Hall's later thinking starts from a specific form of pessimism that bears a strong resemblance to Critical Theory. Especially in his writings during Prime Minister Margaret Thatcher's time in office in the 1980s, Hall refined his method of conjunctural analysis. Based on Italian Marxist Antonio Gramsci's theory of history, class formation and hegemony, Hall's approach also subscribes to Gramsci's demand for an analytical "pessimism of the intelligence, optimism of the will".[4] A similar formulation is occasionally used by Adorno and Horkheimer, especially in their later writings.[5] In Gramsci's thought, pessimism and optimism are political dispositions which can have multiple implications. Shedding light on Gramsci's uses of pessimism and optimism can help to understand the political and intellectual pessimism in the works of Adorno, Horkheimer and Hall.

Gramsci's thinking on the political importance of pessimism and optimism can be traced from his early journalistic writings to his major work, the *Prison Notebooks*. Quite surprising considering his later endorsement of pessimism of the intellect, one of his early articles is titled "Against Pessimism" (1921). In this article, Gramsci takes aim at what he perceives to be the "gravest" danger of his time: the prevalent political pessimism of parts of the newly founded Italian Communist Party (PCI). This pessimism was considered by Gramsci to be a debilitating attitude which would negatively affect the militant project of the new party "because of the political passivity, the intellectual torpor and the scepticism towards the future which they produce".[6] Gramsci associates this pessimism with the stagnant sentiments of the earlier Socialist Party. For Gramsci, the existence of a new party delegitimates pessimism, and he warns against an optimism that only shows in "periods of the fat kine".[7] His later notion of the optimism of the will is prefigured in his call for the "will" that distinguishes the PCI from the traditionalism of the Socialist Party. Gramsci's article, then, is a call for the optimism of the will that is vital especially in a time when the overall situation in the country is marked by a general political pessimism.[8] It is thus "necessary to react forcefully against the pessimism of certain groups within our party"[9] and "to dissipate the dark cloudbanks of pessimism which are today oppressing even the most experienced and responsible militants".[10] Gramsci thus calls for what he will later, in the historical analyses of the *Prison Notebooks*, call a "constructive act of the will".[11]

A different inflection of pessimism and optimism surfaces a few years later in another article, Gramsci's "Address to the Anarchists". This is presumably the first time he uses the phrase "pessimism of the intellect, optimism of the will", attributed to the French writer Romain Rolland.[12] Gramsci accuses the Italian anarchists of "vacuous and pseudo-revolutionary demagogy" and "street-level, simple-minded optimism" which has no answer for the situation of the proletariat which "has been plunged into the deepest abyss of poverty and oppression that the mind of man could ever conceive"—a situation that the "[s]ocialist pessimism" repudiated by the anarchists is better equipped to assess.[13] Gramsci thus distinguishes two kinds of pessimism and optimism. There is a paralysing pessimism which hinders the revolutionary project, and there is a pessimism of the intellect which is an important analytical tool. There is also a "simple-minded" optimism which needs to be replaced with an optimism of the will. This optimism of the will can contain paralysing pessimism, and coupled with the pessimism of the intellect, it will be a revolutionary tool. This, as David Fisher comments on Romain Rolland's original phrase, is a "dialectical blend of negative and positive, realism and idealism, self-knowledge and self-affirmation, linked to a mature historical sense of the possibilities of a rationally organized social community, [which] allows the writer to act, to mediate, to contest, and to dream all at the same time".[14]

Gramsci applies this dialectic to his historical analyses in the *Prison Notebooks*, specifically in "The Modern Prince" and in "The Study of Philosophy". Here, Gramsci challenges linear and teleological narratives of progress which elsewhere he also identifies in the utopian ideas of the Italian anarchists, and which "are incapable of relating means to end, and hence are not even wills, but idle whims, dreams, longings, etc."[15] A "political will" in the proper sense, then, is optimistic, but it can only be truly relevant and effective if it is coupled with a pessimism of the intellect. In short, utopianism is not effective precisely because it does not result from a dialectical relationship between pessimism and optimism and denies an accurate "analysis of situations".[16] This analysis (which is the foundation for Stuart Hall's later conjunctural analyses) must indeed always start with a notion of "becoming" and "dialectical movement" rather than with a "vulgar notion of evolution" to be truly accurate.[17] The notion of crisis that is so central for Gramsci's theory of hegemony stems from the same thought: a linear, evolutionary notion of progress cannot adequately account for the crises that are crucial for understanding historical and political developments as well as the shifts in hegemonic relations. Gramsci's dialectical approach is thus a critical intervention in what he calls "the crisis of the idea of progress".[18] Gramsci's political pessimism thus is a product of his dialectical engagement with history. To be a helpful "realistic description of the status quo",[19] it must avoid being a condition of passivity, and it must never be decoupled from its dialectics with optimism.

Theory and Practice: Horkheimer and Adorno's Critical Theory

A similar dialectics of optimism and pessimism can be found in the work of Max Horkheimer and Theodor Adorno. Contrary to Gramsci's historical materialism, however, Adorno and Horkheimer's engagement with optimism and pessimism, while equally rooted in Marxist thought, is also influenced by the metaphysical pessimism of Arthur Schopenhauer. The latter's influence is particularly prominent in Horkheimer's solo work and mostly retreats into the background in his co-written work with Adorno. Adorno refers to Schopenhauer occasionally, such as throughout his *Minima Moralia*, but Schopenhauer's metaphysical pessimism is an integral part of Max Horkheimer's "intellectual physiognomy".[20] Horkheimer's most explicit engagement with Schopenhauerian philosophy comes into its own especially in his later work. His lecture "Pessimismus heute" ("Pessimism Today") is a prime example. "Pessimism Today" traces pessimist thought from antiquity through the Enlightenment to modernity.[21] The coordinates are the relationship between science, religion and metaphysics. The Enlightenment marks a rupture in the way the world is explained: science and rational thought take the place of religion in making sense of the world, but this does not come without a cost. Reiterating similar arguments found in his book *Eclipse of Reason* and in his collaboration with Theodor Adorno, *Dialectic of Enlightenment*, he points out that it is too short-sighted to believe that the Enlightenment is a one-way road or a linear route to progress and rationality. In fact, rationality, which should empower people to think for themselves and to grasp the world rationally, can turn into its dialectic other: mass deception and unreflected positivism.

For Horkheimer, the history of pessimism is the story of philosophy and its attempt to reconcile science and religion. More precisely, pessimism accounts for philosophy's failure to successfully reconcile science and religion. It accounts for the weakness in the argument of many thinkers who ultimately resort to the explanation of a higher Being whenever they reach the limits of their rational thought. For Horkheimer, Schopenhauer is essential since he acknowledged that the meaning of life is a "hallucination" and puts compassion for the suffering of the other to the fore of his thought: "Pessimismus ist die Negation des Lebenswillens" ("pessimism is the negation of the will to live").[22]

Why does Horkheimer cherish Schopenhauer's ideas? For him, a Schopenhauerian perspective does not shy away from seeing behind the façade of "the good life". He uses the example of the prime ministers of Western countries who smilingly shake the hands of dictators of the political right and left, knowing full well that they are dealing with mass murderers.[23] Shaking hands with those responsible for present-day atrocities, however, is justified by the preservation of the good life in wealthy Western nations: appeasement ensures the safety of the Western people, but it also makes the smiling hand-shakers complicit with these crimes. Horkheimer's engagement with Schopenhauer's pessimism, then, is more than taking up residence in the "Grand Hotel Abyss" to contemplate the miseries of the world from a safe distance, as György Lukács once polemically accused the Frankfurt School of.[24] It is a form of ethical intervention. Pessimism, in this scenario, looks behind the smile and the hand-shaking to reveal its actual motives. It is the negation of the will to live if, as Horkheimer illustrates in his reading of Schopenhauer, the will to live is mere individualist self-preservation.

What Horkheimer identifies in Schopenhauer as one of the core qualities of metaphysical pessimism is an unconditional compassion for the other and their suffering which, sociologically, can be translated into a nonconformist critique of the status quo. Pessimism does not trust the smiles and the hand-shaking. It does not trust rationality as the ultimate good.[25] Crucially, for Horkheimer, the pessimist, who above all things is a thinker capable of compassion, can preserve in the form of culture those Schopenhauerian virtues such as compassion and shared joy ("die für Schopenhauer wesentlichen Tugenden, Mitleid und Mitfreude").[26]

Horkheimer closes his observations on pessimism with the prospect of pessimism, negative thought and their role in Critical Theory. Pessimism is a mode of historical analysis of "past misery, present-day injustice and the prospect of a future devoid of meaning" ("die den vom Elend der Vergangenheit, dem Unrecht der Gegenwart und der Aussicht auf eine des geistigen Sinns entbehrende Zukunft wissenden Menschen").[27] Those who are capable of this awareness reject the claim for absolute truth and focus on a solidarity which is aimed at a better, more compassionate future.

A pessimist ethics is thus integral to the project of Critical Theory which Horkheimer elsewhere defines as the aim to "define the good as the attempt to define evil" as opposed to the morally impossible task to "define evil by the good".[28]

A pessimist theory thus must be coupled with a forward-thinking, pre-figurative mode of practice. His choice of words in the German original is crucial here: "Mit theoretischem Pessimismus könnte eine nicht unoptimistische Praxis sich verbinden, die, des universalen Schlechten eingedenk, das Mögliche trotz allem zu verbessern sucht"—"The pessimism of theory could be coupled with a not unoptimistic practice which, in full awareness of the universal bad, tries to improve the possible against all odds".[29] Grammatically, Horkheimer remains on the pessimist side by using the subjunctive mode and double negation to emphasise the precarious nature of the optimistic ("not unoptimistic") practice, as if he was afraid that too much optimistic faith in practice could veer into the hypocritical smiling and hand-shaking of politicians. Alfred Schmidt detects in this passage the kernel of Horkheimer's late philosophy—"a modest, but humane perspective—a perspective that is oriented analytically toward Marx, metaphysically toward Schopenhauer, and yet transcends them both".[30] Put simply (maybe too simply for his tastes), Horkheimer's idea of the potential of pessimism is clearly aimed at a better world. For him, Critical Theory is a pessimist project, but it is not one devoid of hope for a better future.

Such a hope can, even for Horkheimer and Adorno, take the form of utopian thought. In 1956, Adorno and Horkheimer sat down for a discussion on the relationship of theory and practice. Transcribed by Adorno's wife and collected in the addenda of the German edition of Horkheimer's collected works,[31] this conversation was presumably meant to be turned into a co-written text. It is a distillation of these two thinkers' work, presenting and synergising major theories and arguments which can be found in *Dialectic of Enlightenment*, Adorno's *Negative Dialectics, Minima Moralia* and Horkheimer's *Eclipse of Reason*. Adorno and Horkheimer explore their positions on the state of the contemporary world, global politics in the shadow of Western post-war capitalism, the loss of utopias and the decline of Marxist theory in the time of the Cold War and nuclear threat. The conversation is an entry point into the connection of theory and practice in Critical Theory as well as into the comparison of Critical Theory and cultural studies. In that respect, it is telling that the English translation of the "Diskussion über Theorie und Praxis" was published with the title *Towards a New Manifesto*. The title articulates what Adorno and Horkheimer might have had in mind with the conversation as the starting point for a new book: to translate the intersection between theory and practice envisioned in *The Manifesto of the Communist Party* into the twentieth century and to continue Karl Marx and Friedrich Engels' work of analysing the past and the present to envision a new future. Thus, this conversation is preoccupied with the idea of utopia like only few other texts by Adorno and Horkheimer. However, for Adorno, the outlook is expectedly bleak: "The horror is that for the first time we live in a world in which we can no longer imagine a better one".[32] This statement seems to anticipate a major dictum of the twenty-first-century conjuncture of pessimism: the oft-quoted and modified observation made by Fredric Jameson that, "due to some weakness in our imagination", it is easier "to imagine the thoroughgoing deterioration of the earth and of nature than the breakdown of late capitalism"[33]—an idea that Mark Fisher has described as a state of "capitalist realism".[34] So what use is a debate on theory and practice if you do not believe, as Horkheimer and Adorno categorically proclaim, that "all will be well"?

The aim of Horkheimer and Adorno is to take the loss of utopia as the starting point for their conception of theory and practice. At an early point in the conversation, Horkheimer jokingly mentions that "Teddie wants to rescue a pair of concepts: theory and practice. These concepts are themselves obsolete."[35] Thus, Horkheimer is already pessimistic about the very concept of theory or theory as a practice in a world in which work has become an absolute. Work, as Horkheimer says, has assumed a "godlike status" in the twentieth century and has become "the key to making sure that 'all will be well'".[36] Where does this leave the sociological theorising of Adorno and Horkheimer on the way to a "New Manifesto"? It lies precisely in the deconstruction of the very idea of work as an ideology of self-fulfilment and being well. In a world in which utopia has been replaced with the deluded idea that work will be the path to happiness, the first step is to rigorously critique and dismantle the dominant notions of happiness, "being well" and optimism. Adorno already elaborated on this in an aphorism[37] in his *Minima Moralia*, titled "Deviation". He takes to task the "hurrah-optimism"[38] of his time which he not only observes in the status quo of a ruling class but equally in the contemporary left. This compulsive and obligatory optimism, Adorno argues, is directly linked to the loss of a true utopian vision:

The constantly enforced insistence that everybody should admit that everything will turn out well, places those who do not under suspicion of being
defeatists and deserters. [...] The optimism of the left repeats the insidious
bourgeois superstition that one should not talk of the devil but look on the
bright side.[39]

Adorno's bleak diagnosis is that even left resistance and the worker struggle have fallen for the same kind of unconditional optimism that is integral
to the bourgeoisie's ideology of work and entrepreneurialism. The revolutionary gestures of the left thus become a revolution without the revolution, or at least without a utopian prospect. The task of theory and critical
thought, then, must be to resist this ubiquitous kind of empty optimism.
In contrast to "hurrah-optimism", then, pessimism becomes not only a
"deviant" but a potentially revolutionary gesture. This subversive pessimism can expose the dialectics of the contemporary world. As he elabo-
rates in his conversation with Horkheimer, reason itself must become the
object of scrutiny to dislodge it from its dialectic other in the age of reason
and machinery: "Reason, which is essential to keep the machinery in
motion, necessarily contains its other. When you start to think, you cannot
stop short at purely reproductive thinking. This does not mean that things
will really work out like that, but you cannot think without thinking that
otherness."[40]

This argument is an echo of Horkheimer's earlier *Eclipse of Reason*.
Written under the acute impression of the Second World War and the
Holocaust, Horkheimer's book addresses the precarious nature of progress and the loss of utopias. Progress and reason have, in Horkheimer's
diagnosis, developed from their original aims during the age of enlightenment into ends in themselves, and critical thought, the imagination and
humanist ideals have been diminished in the process. Thought itself has
become integrated into the capitalist logic of production and consumption: "Concepts have become 'streamlined,' rationalized, labor-saving
devices. It is as if thinking itself had been reduced to the level of industrial
processes, subjected to a close schedule—in short, made part and parcel of
production."[41]

Horkheimer criticises the devaluation and emptying of theory and its
subjection to the dogma of use value:

In order to prove its right to be conceived, each thought must have an alibi,
must present a record of its expediency. Even if its direct use is 'theoretical,'

it is ultimately put to test by the practical application of the theory in which it functions. Thought must be gauged by something that is not thought, by its effect on production or its impact on social conduct, as art today is ultimately being gauged in every detail by something that is not art, be it box-office or propaganda value.[42]

Optimism becomes an expression of the general inability to actually face the conditions of modernity: "This comes to the fore in many ethical or religious discussions in pragmatist writings. They are liberal, tolerant, optimistic, and quite unable to deal with the cultural debacle of our days."[43] Thus, quite paradoxically, optimism becomes a paralysing rather than a motivating and forward-moving disposition. Even more dramatically, this kind of optimism is directly linked to the paradox of mass society in which "the masses", rather than being mobilised as a collectivity, are encouraged to resort to individualist perspectives, atomising society and preventing progressive thought and action:

Today, progress toward utopia is blocked primarily by the complete dispro-portion between the weight of the overwhelming machinery of social power and that of the atomized masses. [...]. The method of negation, the denunciation of everything that mutilates mankind and impedes its free develop-ment, rests on the confidence of man. [...]. If by enlightenment and intellectual progress we mean the freeing of man from superstitious belief in evil forces, in demons and fairies, in blind fate—in short, the emancipation from fear—then denunciation of what is currently called reason is the greatest service reason can render.[44]

Does this mean that the project of Critical Theory is content with ruthlessly pointing out and criticising notions of happiness and optimism in their complicity with ideology? Certainly not—in fact, they point out that the notion of utopia remains vital and must be an integral part of every critical thought process: "The general stultification today is the direct result of cutting out utopia. When you reject utopia, thought itself withers away. Thought is killed off in the mere doubling process."[45] Utopia emerges as a central element of critical thought, but at the same time it involves the danger of reducing its own ideas to a "theory that does not lead to action"—a theory which one arrives at when "one always refers back to the idea of measuring everything according to the image of how one would like things to be".[46] This idea is similar to Gramsci's concerns about the utopian socialists of his own time, who promote an optimistic vision of the future which is not grounded in a rigorous analysis of real historical conditions. Consequently, Horkheimer and Adorno contend that "[r]eality should be measured against criteria whose capacity for fulfilment can be demonstrated in a number of already existing, concrete developments in historical reality".[47] In contrast (or in addition) to this notion of utopia as pure theory, Adorno adds that for him, "[t]heory is already practice. And practice presupposes theory."[48]

So utopia is theory—and likewise, the very ability to think and theorise can be utopian. For Horkheimer, it is an antidote to his general pessimism: "The only thing that goes against my pessimism is the fact that we still carry on thinking today. All hope lies in thought. But it is easy to believe that it could all come to an end."[49] Against the imminent threat of the end, "our task is at the very least to bring out the utopia in the negative picture".[50] Thus, Adorno and Horkheimer's pessimism, unlike that of many other pessimists who have addressed utopia, such as E. M. Cioran and John Gray,[51] does not feel content with deconstructing and rejecting utopianism as a delusional fantasy that has replaced religious hopes for salvation. It in fact *requires* utopia as a horizon against which to measure its critique of reality. Thus, to come back to the notion of dialectics so central to the project of Critical Theory, pessimism and utopia must form a dialectic if both are to fulfil their tasks.

CULTURAL STUDIES: STUART HALL'S CONJUNCTURAL ANALYSIS AS PESSIMIST METHOD

The inception of Cultural studies in Britain marked a change in theorising the complex intersections of society, politics, media and cultural production. Stuart Hall emerged as one of the central theorists of the Birmingham Centre for Contemporary Cultural Studies. His thinking is informed by Marxism, sociology and the theorising of ethnicity and difference. A prolific writer since the 1950s, Hall was an acute observer of the cultural and political formations in Britain after the Second World War. When Conservative Prime Minister Margaret Thatcher came to power in 1979, Hall became one of the most incisive commentators on the political shift to the right that would mark 1980s Britain—the decade was, as the title of one of his essays said, "The Great Moving Right Show".[52] His book *The Long Hard Road to Renewal* is a collection of his essays on the period of Thatcher's three legislatures up until 1990, and it is the one in which his call for the method of conjunctural analysis is most pronounced. The book takes a Gramscian approach to Thatcherism and considers it as an ideological response to the organic and conjunctural crises of post-war Britain. The major characteristics of these crises are the shifting balance between Britain's two major parties, the Conservative Party and the Labour Party, and their respective voter bases. This political shift is mainly a crisis of socialism and traditional working-class politics. As the British working class increasingly diversified and stratified internally, alienation between Labour and its voters became more and more dramatic. At the same time, Thatcher's conservative politics became the hegemonic response to the conjunctural crisis of the 1980s.[53] For Hall, and especially for his former students such as Lawrence Grossberg, who contributed significantly to shaping the concept for present-day cultural studies, conjunctural analysis is one of the major tasks of cultural studies. As I pointed out in the introduction to this book, the aim of conjunctural analysis is the comprehensive understanding of hegemonic cultural and political formations of a historical moment and its temporality. Hall was never content to remain in the past or present tense, though. For him, conjunctural analysis must always be utilised to prepare action for the future. Thus, cultural studies is a discipline that is always operating in the "future tense".[54]

The relationship of cultural studies to temporalities and its conception of conjunctural analysis are therefore the aspects that are most directly linked to notions of pessimism and optimism. For Grossberg, conjunctural analysis itself is the method that embodies the Gramscian pessimism of the intellect in its analytical assessment of the conditions of an epoch and the optimism of the will in the resulting action. This action may consist of, among other things, "imagin[ing] the possibility of multiple ways of being"[55] and of finding "re-articulations of the old with the new".[56] Conjunctural analysis, in its movement from theory to practice, is directly engaging in a Gramscian struggle over hegemony: "It is this focus on struggle and process—the dialectic between maps and stories in the constant recalibration of contingency and actuality—that enables cultural studies to move from pessimism to optimism".[57] Pessimism and optimism are here part of the "affective landscapes" of a conjuncture.[58] For Grossberg, who updates Hall's conjunctural analysis for the twenty-first-century conjuncture—with the rise of Trump and other new right figures—the 2010s are a conjuncture marked by pessimist and nihilist affect, as opposed to the optimism of a period such as the 1960s. However, with his sight firmly set on the future, conjunctural analysis must never stop at dwelling on the "organization of pessimism" of a given conjuncture but must work towards imagining better worlds. Here, the utopian aspect of cultural studies comes into view—an aspect that Grossberg and later John Storey[59] have emphasised.

But what did the pessimism of the intellect and the optimism of the will concretely look like in Hall's own work? For Hall, the notions of pessimism and optimism emerge from his deep engagement with Gramsci's political thought and the question how Gramsci's concept could be productively used to make sense of the political situation in Britain in the 1980s. For Hall, "Thatcherism" was not only a mere phase of the Conservative Party government but the result of a more wide-ranging shift to the right. The "Great Moving Right Show" was a hegemonic shift in politics, society, economics and culture. Thus, the analysis of the conjuncture also requires a critical self-assessment of the contemporary left and its ability to challenge Thatcher's hegemony.

This is most pronounced in the essay "Gramsci and Us", which addresses the potential and limits of Gramsci's thought. Hall's approach to a Gramscian mode of analysis avoids the deception that Gramsci offers ready-made concepts that would function as a one-size-fits-all explanatory model: "We can't pluck up this 'Sardinian' from his specific and unique political formation, beam him down at the end of the twentieth century, and ask him to solve our problems for us: especially since the whole thrust of his thinking was to refuse this easy transfer of generalisations from one conjuncture, nation or epoch to another."[60] The challenge of conjunctural analysis, then, is to avoid the temptation to think in simplified historical continuities. Rather, conjunctural analysis must use Gramscian tools to identify and describe not the similarities between different historical moments but what is unique about a given conjuncture: "So, instead of asking 'what would Gramsci say about Thatcherism?' we should simply attend to this riveting of Gramsci to the notion of difference, to the specificity of a historical conjuncture: how different forces come together, conjuncturally, to create the new terrain, on which a different politics must form up."[61] This is where Hall takes up the Gramscian phrase of pessimism of the intellect, optimism of the will: "[w]hen a conjuncture unrolls, there is no 'going back'. History shifts gears. The terrain changes. You are in a new moment. You have to attend, 'violently', with all the 'pessimism of the intellect' at your command, to the 'discipline of the conjuncture.'"[62]

The pessimism of the intellect, then, is a rigorous pessimism of analysis. It tends to the current historical moment and subjects it to scrutiny. For an intellectual project that is not only devoted to a distanced analysis of a situation but also seeks alternatives to it, however, the pessimism of the intellect is on the other hand also a pessimism about the analyser and their methods. In other words, it is a political pessimism that identifies the problems and challenges of a conjuncture, but it also is a pessimism about the possibilities and limits of conjunctural analysis and about the possibility of political change itself. It is, however, not a defeatist pessimism, since it is paired with the optimism of the will which is aimed beyond the time of the conjuncture and looks towards the future. Conjunctural analysis, in its intellectual pessimism, then, is rooted in the assessment of and confrontation with the worst. At the same time, it is balanced with an optimism that is based on identifying the options for progressive action that are left after this assessment of the worst. In other words, the optimism of the will mines the possibilities left for imagining better futures: "In front of us is the historic choice: capitulate to the Thatcherite future, or find another way of imagining".[63]

What is crucial for the left's ability to figure out paths for the future after Thatcherism, though, is to be as radical in its critical self-assessment as in its analysis of Thatcherism. This also means to acknowledge the fact that "a tiny bit of all of us is also in the Thatcherist project".[64] The pessimism of the intellect thus must also be aimed at oneself as a means of ideological introspection. For how else would a hegemonic project be able to establish itself if not for the substantial ideological support in the whole cultural arena? It is precisely because Thatcherism articulates tendencies inherent in a majority of the population during a given conjuncture that it is able to maintain its hegemony. To explain this with a more contemporary analogy, one could turn to the way the contemporary left is not exempt from the notions of neoliberal entrepreneurship, as can be seen in the accelerationist movement which to some degree radically and unabashedly affirms aspects of neoliberalism in its belief to bring neoliberalism to its knees. Hall himself jokingly mentions the conspicuous consumption habits which unite social democrats and Tory Thatcherites.[65] This unscrupulous introspection of the British left is necessary to set sight on political and cultural realities because "[w]histling in the dark is an occupational hazard not altogether unknown on the British left".[66] Hall rejects a "revolutionary optimism" with which parts of the left urge themselves to "look for the points of resistance" and that they "will rise again"—rather, "if we are to be effective, politically, it can only be on the basis of a serious analysis of things as they are, not as we would wish them to be".[67] This rejection of false hopes as a denial of the present is what for Hall epitomises the Gramscian pessimism of the intellect. It is also where Hall's political thinking shares similarities with Gramsci's and Adorno and Horkheimer's critique of a utopian optimism that is not grounded in historical analysis.

What can be seen in the way Hall approaches his Gramscian analysis of the conjuncture of Thatcherism is that pessimism and optimism pertain to two different levels. First, they relate both to the way the temporality of a conjuncture is lived and experienced by the cultural actors of that conjuncture (i.e., how temporality is experienced in Britain during 1980s Thatcherism) and to the way the analyst describes and interprets the temporality of a conjuncture in comparison and in historical context, with both a view to the past and to the possible futures after the conjuncture. This entails, among others, to question how Gramsci's notions of organic and conjunctural crisis as developed in his writings on Fascist Italy relate to 1980s Britain under Thatcher. This, as Hall stresses, does not mean to draw continuities or analogies. Rather, Gramsci's concepts must adapt to the new cultural and historical context. Second, the conjuncture itself always effectively plays out along the lines of optimism and pessimism.

Lawrence Grossberg later elaborated on this aspect. In his work, which primarily focuses on describing the conjuncture of US politics and culture since the 1990s with a focus on the era of George W. Bush and Donald Trump, Grossberg asks what structure of feeling towards the future a conjuncture is dominated by. He contrasts the 1960s which were largely dominated by "organizations of optimism", even if this was articulated differently across sectors of the culture in what he describes as a "paradoxical temporality", from a dominant conformist mainstream culture to the counterculture.[68] In contrast, the period from the 1990s to the 2010s was marked by "organizations of pessimism": faith in progress and the future gave way to cynicism, irony, relativism and an anxiety whose "object is time itself", culminating in "temporal alienation".[69]

Grossberg adapts the concept of "organization of pessimism" versus "organization of optimism" from Walter Benjamin, who in his 1929 essay on French surrealism challenged what he perceived to be the optimism of a bourgeois social-democratic leftism which indulges in "stock images" of a happy future for all, a "bad poem on springtime, filled to bursting with metaphors".[70] In Benjamin's appropriation of surrealism, pessimism becomes the necessary response to bourgeois social-democratic politics that fails to move beyond symbolic moralistic gestures instead of actual revolution. A "pessimism all along the line"[71] must be the answer to the false hopes articulated by both the bourgeois left as well as capitalism itself.[72]

What Benjamin envisions, then, is a pessimism that serves as a means of enlightenment and emancipation, while optimism merely represents the hopeful delusions of bourgeois ideology. Benjamin's thinking about surrealism as a pessimist aesthetic-political revolutionary project is close to Hall's Gramscian refusal to buy into the cheerful, yet delusional optimistic projections of a better future for the left in the face of Thatcherism and the erosion of a coherent socialism in the 1980s Britain. In other words, for both Benjamin and Hall (as well as for Gramsci in a different historical context), hope (and optimism) can never be enough. Merely hoping for a better future entails the risk of being passive in the face of the challenges of the present. It is in this sentiment that cultural studies, Critical Theory and Gramscian theory come full circle. Horkheimer and Adorno share with Benjamin and Hall a deep scepticism about a politics of optimism, which does not mean that they did not have visions for a better—maybe even utopian—future. Rather, as can be seen in Adorno and Horkheimer's discussion about theory and practice, utopia must be considered a vital aspect of critique—an aspect which I will return to shortly in my discussion of John Storey's radical utopianism. They envisioned Critical Theory as an ongoing intervention into whatever the prevailing optimistic narrative of the day was. As can be seen in both Adorno and Horkheimer's writings, and especially in Horkheimer's engagement with Schopenhauer, their pessimism of theory is also a necessary ethical intervention that deconstructs the false morals of organisations of optimism. Pessimism, understood in this way, becomes an ethical mode of critique.

The pessimism of the intellect that unites all these thinkers shares the notion of what I have called "precarious temporality".[73] In Hall's Gramscian thinking, crisis becomes the dominant temporal paradigm. This crisis, whether it is organic or conjunctural, is caused by a multiplicity of factors which in the political arena amount to a "broken dialogue between socialism and modernity".[74] Likewise, Wendy Brown has described crisis as a "rupture of temporal continuity" and marks a situation in which "time itself lacks its capacity to contain us and conjoin us".[75] Crisis lays bare the precarious nature of time in that it demonstrates the different and sometimes contingent time-scales which mark our sense of time. A crisis marks the loss of a sense of future and turns time into an "unbearable present" that entraps a polity and robs it of a vision for the future.[76] It is important to emphasise here that Brown points to the shared etymological roots of the terms "crisis" and "critique", the Greek term *krisis*.[77] In its original form, the term means "discrimination" or "distinction", and was later used to name the crucial turning point during which a critical condition can lead to an illness getting either better or worse.[78] This is the shared meaning of critique and crisis: both challenge and disrupt notions of temporality. For Brown, critique arises as an answer to a political crisis and exposes it as a rupture of political time. In that, critique is always "untimely" in that it is seemingly voiced at an inopportune moment. Thus, it could be argued that critique is always inherently pessimist since pessimism questions or negates dominant notions of temporality and narratives of progress. Critique and pessimism are disruptive. The time is never right for either critique or pessimism—unlike the motivational mode of optimism, "no one needs pessimism" and "no one has time for pessimism", as Eugene Thacker aptly observes.[79] Hall, Horkheimer and Adorno's pessimism of the intellect is particularly untimely and uncalled for since it aims not only at political and ideological opponents but also at their own oppositional political projects. Both the thinkers of the Frankfurt School and Hall use pessimism as a meta-critical mode. While Horkheimer and Adorno are facing the corruption and failure of the socialist project in post-war Europe as well as the unbroken prevailing of the Enlightenment project in the form of "instrumental reason" (Horkheimer), Hall confronts the failure of the British left to formulate a sustained counter-hegemonic programme to challenge Thatcher's neoliberal politics. What is left hanging in the air, however, is the notion of utopia. If, as Horkheimer and Adorno argue, utopia is the pre-requisite for true critical thought, then how can utopia be reconciled with the pessimism of the intellect?

Hope After Pessimism? Utopia Today

After the pessimist analysis has tended "violently" to the conjuncture and after every ethical blind spot, every hypocrisy, every "doubling of the world"[80] has been subjected to thorough critical analysis, what is there left to believe in? What political projects and what visions of a future society can be formulated—what object is the optimism of the will and of practice left with? Can hope be restored as an affect and as a prefigurative outlook on the future after the pessimist intellect has done away with all false illusions? It might be tempting to resort to a cosmic-pessimist perspective and wonder what E. M. Cioran, Thomas Ligotti or Eugene Thacker might have to say about hope. Does a pessimist analysis of the way things are not ultimately lead to "infinite resignation", with pessimism as a "theory of 'giving up'"?[81] Reading Stuart Hall nursing his "election blues" in the afterthoughts to each devastating Tory election victory throughout the 1980s, a pessimist might be compelled to respond with Eugene Thacker's resigned aphorism: "I no longer want to hear about how your revolution failed. Again."[82] After all, to continue in the Thackerian vein, "[t]here is no better occasion for pessimism than optimism".[83] The question, then, is whether hope after pessimism is still possible, or rather, whether the two can be reconciled. At this point it is worth returning to Horkheimer's reading of Schopenhauer which he concludes by saying "[t]here are few ideas that the world today needs more than Schopenhauer's—ideas which in the face of utter hopelessness, because they confront it, know more than any others of hope".[84] A Schopenhauerian kind of hope as Horkheimer envisions it could be called a hopeless hope because it rejects the hopeful and illusory promise of compensation in the beyond of the afterlife and lets one realise one's abandonment. It is this sense of abandonment that can become the motor for solidarity "in *this* world"—and this is a solidarity that "stems from hopelessness".[85]

Hope and solidarity that result from or in the face of hopelessness might sound paradoxical or counterintuitive. And yet, the sociologist Shona Hunter, in her analysis of agency and affect of actors in institutional spaces in contemporary Britain, proposes a similar theory. In many ways, Hunter's approach is in the vein of conjunctural analysis. She provides an account of governance in the neoliberal era since the election of New Labour's Prime Minister Tony Blair in 1997. Starting from the young Prime Minister's "heady optimism" apparent in his speeches in which he declared that "fear lost" and "[h]ope won",[86] Hunter asks what narratives of hope are co-opted and by whom. If the newly elected government claims for itself the power of hope and delineates a seemingly linear and clear route for social and economic progress, then where does this leave social entities reliant on institutional spaces such as the National Health Service who might feel abandoned by precisely these institutions?

Hunter highlights experiences of difference within institutions that undermine the homogeneous and streamlined narrative of Blairite optimism and identifies in these experiences feelings of loss and the melancholia of failed mourning that result from the absence of a shared reality: "a shared reality exists only in so far as it is signed up to and invested in by differentiated subjects. Therefore, it only exists in so far as the desire for contact and understanding between subjects is hoped for."[87] Hunter's examination of "a conflicted institutional space characterized by internal crisis",[88] in its focus on moments of crisis, works like Gramscian conjunctural analysis and equally rejects the Blairite organisation of optimism. However, she does not stop at the deconstruction and rejection of false ideological optimism but works towards a rearticulation of hope. She highlights negative affects like loss and melancholia as reactions to the failure of individuals and institutions as conditions for the "radical everyday" as "disruptive force".[89] This disruption can facilitate "a realistically reconstructive critique of the state that provides hope for change in the face of loss".[90] Her theorisation of what she calls "reality's unreality" is crucial for this critique—a critique that will ultimately produce new forms of resistant hope within and against institutional spaces. This entails working against the "illusory nature of reality"—the condition that one can never fully know another's reality. The "act of hoping", Hunter argues, can have the potential to unite individuals in the expectation of a mutually shared reality—even in the face of the potential failure of such an endeavour. This kind of melancholic hope, then, is reclaiming and reappropriating the very concept and potential of hope from the hegemonic forces of the state. This kind of hope which could be labelled "hegemonic hope" is indeed the "hopeful expectation that one will change" that Slavoj Žižek would criticise as that which "is exactly what obstructs change".[91]

This notion of hope as opposition in the face of failure, which is also a practice of solidarity that resists the de-solidarity of the state and its institutions, bears resemblance to the "melancholic hope" that Mathias Thaler sees as the potential product of engaging with dystopian narratives which "defamiliarize" the present[92] and which foster a "strategic combination of hope and despair".[93] It seems, then, that a true hope that can actually serve as an empowering affect that constitutes agency and triggers change, cannot be had without a suitable mode of pessimist analysis. What is also at stake in this notion of hope is that it needs to address the nature of "reality". This does not mean, however, that this type of hope is merely one that is to be taken as the "more realistic" and therefore modest kind of optimism. Rather, Hunter and Thaler's notions of melancholic hope resemble what John Storey has outlined as "radical utopianism". Storey considers radical utopianism as a tool of "defamiliarization"—"the making strange of what currently exists in order to dislodge its taken-for-grantedness and in so doing make possible the production of utopian desire" and thus "offers a challenge to our complicity with power".[94] Like Hunter's illusory unreality, Storey's radical utopianism is a way to intervene in the "manufactured naturalness of the here and now".[95] Storey draws on Ernst Bloch's concept of "educated hope"[96] as the motor for producing a desire for going beyond what is hegemonically considered to be possible or "realistic". He describes as "impossibilism" the hegemonic way of defining what "reality" is and what is possible and impossible within the limits of that "reality".[97] Defamiliarisation through radical utopianism thus means to denaturalise the boundaries of "reality", much like Hunter's melancholic hope. It is also, as Storey argues in his book, a way to realise the political promises of early British cultural studies. Storey returns to early texts by two of the founding figures of cultural studies, the Marxist historian E. P. Thompson and the cultural critic Raymond Williams, who have in various places of their work written on utopianism. Thompson saw his own approach to a "history from below" as a way to unearth the radical utopian potential in hitherto historically neglected early working-class movements and wrote extensively on the utopian writer William Morris, while Raymond Williams was a prolific scholar of utopian science fiction literature. Storey's *Radical Utopianism and Cultural Studies*, in its attempt to bring together historical examples of fully realised utopianism, with the theories of cultural studies, is then a late response to the open questions about the optimism of the will of Hall's and Grossberg's conjunctural analyses.

Notes

1. Max Horkheimer and Theodor Adorno, *Dialectic of Enlightenment: Philosophical Fragments* (Redwood: Stanford University Press, 2002).
2. Raymond Williams, *The Long Revolution* (Cardigan: Parthian, 2013), p. 67.
3. John Storey, *Cultural Studies and the Study of Popular Culture* (Edinburgh: Edinburgh University Press, 2010), p. 140.
4. Stuart Hall, *The Hard Road to Renewal. Thatcherism and the Crisis of the Left* (London: Verso, 2021), p. 42.
5. See for instance Max Horkheimer, "Pessimismus Heute", in *Sozialphilosophische Studien: Aufsätze, Reden und Vorträge 1930–1972*, ed. Werner Brede (Frankfurt am Main: Fischer, 1972), 137–44, p. 143.
6. Antonio Gramsci, *Selections from Political Writings, 1921–1926* (London: Lawrence and Wishart, 1978), p. 213.
7. Gramsci, 1978, p. 213.
8. Gramsci, 1978, p. 213.

9. Gramsci, 1978, p. 216.
10. Gramsci, 1978, p. 213.
11. Antonio Gramsci, *Selections from the Prison Notebooks* (London: Lawrence & Wishart, 2003), p. 174.
12. Antonio Gramsci, *Selections from Political Writings, 1910–1920* (London: Lawrence and Wishart, 1977), p. 188.
13. Gramsci, 1977, p. 188.
14. David James Fisher, *Romain Rolland and the Politics of Intellectual Engagement* (Berkeley: University of California Press, 1988), p. 302.
15. Gramsci, 2003, p. 175.
16. Gramsci, 2003, p. 175.
17. Gramsci, 2003, p. 358.
18. Gramsci, 2003, p. 358.
19. Franscesca Antonini, 'Pessimism of the Intellect, Optimism of the Will: Gramsci's Political Thought in the Last Miscellaneous Notebooks', *Rethinking Marxism* 31, no. 1 (2019): 42–57, p. 42.
20. Alfred Schmidt, 'Max Horkheimer's Intellectual Physiognomy', in *On Max Horkheimer: New Perspectives*, ed. Seyla Benhabib, Wolfgang Bonss, and John McCole (Cambridge, Mass.: MIT Press, 1993), 25–48, p. 25.
21. Max Horkheimer, 'Pessimismus heute', in *Sozialphilosophische Studien: Aufsätze, Reden nnd Vorträge 1930–1972*, ed. Werner Brede (Frankfurt am Main: Fischer, 1972), 137–44.
22. Horkheimer, 1972, p. 140.
23. Horkheimer, 1972, p. 140.
24. Qtd. in Stuart Jeffries. *Grand Hotel Abyss: The Lives of the Frankfurt School.* (London: Verso, 2017), p. 1.
25. Horkheimer, 1972, p. 142.
26. Horkheimer, 1972, p. 142.
27. Horkheimer, 192, p. 143.
28. Max Horkheimer, *Dawn & Decline: Notes 1926–1931 and 1950–1969* (New York: The Seabury Press, 1978), p. 237.
29. Horkheimer, 1972, p. 143.
30. Schmidt, 1993, p. 40.
31. Max Horkheimer and Theodor W. Adorno, 'Diskussion über Theorie und Praxis', in *Max Horkheimer: Gesammelte Schriften*, ed. Gunzelin Schmid Noerr, vol. 19 (Frankfurt am Main: Fischer, 1996), 32–71.
32. Theodor Adorno and Max Horkheimer, *Towards a New Manifesto* (London: Verso, 2019), p. 72.
33. Fredric Jameson, *The Seeds of Time* (New York: Columbia University Press, 1994), p. xii.
34. Mark Fisher, *Capitalist Realism. Is There No Alternative?* (Winchester: Zero, 2009), p. 2.

35. Adorno & Horkheimer, 2019, p. 13.
36. Adorno & Horkheimer, 2019, p. 7.
37. For discussions of Adorno and his use of aphorism as pessimist form, see Joshua Foa Dienstag, *Pessimism: Philosophy, Ethic, Spirit* (New Jersey: Princeton University Press, 2006),
38. pp. 227–228; see also Eugene Thacker, *Cosmic Pessimism* (Minneapolis: Univocal, 2015), pp. 54–55; *Infinite Resignation* (London: Repeater, 2018), p. 263.
39. Theodor Adorno, *Minima Moralia: Reflections from Damaged Life* (London: Verso, 2020), p. 122.
40. Adorno, 2020, p. 122.
41. Adorno & Horkheimer, 2019, p. 3.
42. Max Horkheimer, *Eclipse of Reason* (London, New York: Bloomsbury, 2013), p. 13.
43. Horkheimer, 2013, p. 34.
44. Horkheimer, 2013, p. 35.
45. Horkheimer, 2013, p. 132.
46. Adorno & Horkheimer, 2019, p. 3.
47. Adorno & Horkheimer, 2019, p. 60.
48. Adorno & Horkheimer, p. 60.
49. Adorno & Horkheimer, 2019, p. 72
50. Adorno & Horkheimer, 2019, p. 27.
51. Adorno & Horkheimer, 2019, p. 42.
    E. M. Cioran, *History and Utopia* (New York: Arcade, 2015); John Gray, *Black Mass: Apocalyptic Religion and the Death of Utopia* (Penguin, 2008). See also Chap. 3 in the present book for a discussion of Cioran's anti-utopianism.
52. Hall, 2021, p. 39.
53. Hall, 2021, p. 179.
54. Lawrence Grossberg, *Cultural Studies in the Future Tense* (Durham: Duke University Press, 2010).
55. Lawrence Grossberg, 'Cultural Studies in Search of a Method, or Looking for Conjunctural Analysis', *New Formations* 96, no. 96 (26 July 2019): 38–68, p. 67.
56. Grossberg, 2019, p. 46.
57. Grossberg, 2019, p. 60.
58. Grossberg, 2019, p. 65.
59. John Storey, *Radical Utopianism and Cultural Studies: On Refusing to Be Realistic* (London, New York: Routledge, 2019).
60. Hall, 2021, p. 161.
61. Hall, 2021, p. 163.
62. Hall, 2021, p. 162.
63. Hall, 2021, p. 172.

64. Hall, 2021, p. 165.
65. Hall, 2021, p. 165.
66. Hall, 2021, pp. 41–42.
67. Hall, 2021, p. 41.
68. Grossberg and Behrenshausen, 2016, p. 1023.
69. Grossberg and Behrenshausen, 2016, p. 1023.
70. Walter Benjamin, 'Surrealism: The Last Snapshot of the European Intelligentsia', *New Left Review*, no. 108 (1978): 47–56, p. 55.
71. Benjamin, 1978, p. 55.
72. Simon Wortham, *Hope: The Politics of Optimism* (London, New York: Bloomsbury, 2020), p. 84.
73. Mark Schmitt, 'Beyond the Future: Crisis and Precarious Temporality in Post-Capitalist Discourse', *Journal for the Study of British Cultures* 24, no. 2 (2018): 189–203.
74. Stuart Hall, 'The Meaning of New Times', in *Critical Dialogues in Cultural Studies*, ed. Kuan-Hsing Chen Morley, David (London: Routledge, 1996), 222–36, p. 231.
75. Wendy Brown, *Edgework. Critical Essays on Knowledge and Politics* (New Jersey: Princeton University Press, 2009), pp. 7–8
76. Brown, 2009, p. 11.
77. Brown, 2009, p. 5.
78. Brown, 2009, p. 5. Cf. also Mark Schmitt, 'Riots: Crowds, Bodies, Temporalities, Utopias', *Coils of the Serpent: Journal for the Study of Contemporary Power*, no. 7 (2020): 73–87.
79. Thacker, Eugene. *Cosmic Pessimism* (Minneapolis: Univocal, 2015), p. 4.
80. Adorno and Horkheimer, 2019, p. 1.
81. Thacker, 2018, p. 51.
82. Thacker, 2018, p. 72.
83. Thacker, 2018, p. 61.
84. Max Horkheimer, *Critique of Instrumental Reason* (London: Verso, 2012), p. 83.
85. Horkheimer, 2012, p. 82.
86. Qtd. in Shona Hunter, *Power, Politics and the Emotions: Impossible Governance?* (Abingdon: Routledge, 2015), p. 3.
87. Hunter, 2015, p. 176.
88. Hunter, 2015, p. 174.
89. Hunter, 2015, p. 175.
90. Hunter, 2015, p. 171.
91. Wortham, 2020, p. 96. See also Slavoj Žižek, *The Courage of Hopelessness: Chronicles of a Year Acting Dangerously* (London: Penguin, 2018).
92. Mathias Thaler, 'Bleak Dreams, Not Nightmares', *Constellations* 26, no. 4 (December 2019): 607–22, p. 612.

93. Thaler, 2019, p. 610.
94. John Storey, *Radical Utopianism and Cultural Studies: On Refusing to Be Realistic* (Abingdon: Routledge, 2019), p. 1
95. Storey, 2019, p. 2.
96. Storey, 2019, p. 5.
97. Storey, 2019, p. 7.

CHAPTER 3

Undoing Better Worlds: Anti-Utopianism from Cioran to Afropessimism

Abstract Anti-utopianist critique is one of the key elements of modern pessimism, with the French-Romanian writer E. M. Cioran being one of the most prominent anti-utopian polemicists. And yet, as Caroline Edwards and Fredric Jameson have argued, a seemingly prevalent scepticism towards utopianism is increasingly being challenged by a prevalent "anti-anti-utopianism". John Storey's concept of "radical utopianism" offers a recent rebuke to pessimism and "impossibilism". This chapter engages with Cioran's critique of utopia and contrasts it with Storey's use of utopianism in the context of cultural studies. The chapter will then link these contrasting arguments with an exploration of two strands of utopian and pessimist imaginations that are representative of the current conjuncture: afropessimism and afrofuturism/Black utopia. An interpretation of John Akomfrah's afrofuturist essay film *The Last Angel of History* (1996) and Steve McQueen's short film "Education" from his anthology *Small Axe* (2020) illustrates the dialectic relationship of afropessimism with notions of (Black) utopia. The chapter thus argues that utopianism and pessimism can be seen as two different and sometimes even complimentary epistemological frames. Thinking pessimism and utopianism as an open-ended, productive dialectic, offers new ways to rethink progress, politics and institutions of care.

© The Author(s), under exclusive license to Springer Nature
Switzerland AG 2023
M. Schmitt, *Spectres of Pessimism*,
https://doi.org/10.1007/978-3-031-25351-5_3

Keywords Utopia • Anti-utopianism • Afropessimism • Afrofuturism • E.M. Cioran • John Storey • Frank B. Wilderson III. • Steve McQueen • John Akomfrah

AGAINST UTOPIANISM

Utopianism is intricately linked with pessimist thought. Pessimist thinkers such as E. M. Cioran and John Gray have notoriously derided the utopian imagination.[1] As several scholars of utopianism have observed, the twentieth and twenty-first centuries have been marked by a prevailing sense of what Caroline Edwards calls a "barrage of anti-utopian censure".[2] E. M. Cioran's pessimist polemic "Mechanism of Utopia" is an example of this anti-utopianism. Taking aim at the allegedly superficial and naïve vision of human character in classic literary utopias, Cioran derided the utopian imagination as a secular substitute for the waning power of religions. Writing in the early twenty-first century and reacting to the threat of Islamist terrorism and the equally fanatic US-American War on Terror, John Gray reiterated this criticism of utopianism as a new form of eschatology.[3] Edwards and other scholars of utopianism challenge such standard anti-utopian reflexes and argue that the utopian imagination comes in much more diverse and complex forms than many of its critics tend to acknowledge, and that we can presently detect a new surge in the utopian imagination. This new utopian tendency is not confined to the literary imagination. Eric Olin Wright, Ruth Levitas and Davina Cooper have explored "real utopias" and how they manifest in a range of sites through cultural and social practices and grassroots politics.[4] Similarly, John Storey argued for what he calls "radical utopianism" for the field of cultural studies, exploring historical examples of utopian moments that bring about a defamiliarisation of the ideological status quo of the present. In these examples, we can see a tendency towards what Caroline Edwards and Fredric Jameson have called a "project of 'anti-anti-utopianism'".[5] This new anti-anti-utopianism is also articulated in often ambiguous contemporary utopian imaginations. As Edwards argues, "[u]topianism and dystopianism are therefore closely linked: what speculative visions of the worst possible society and the best possible society share is a critique of the author's (and the contemporary reader's) own socio-political world. Dystopian fiction is not anti-utopian, since the underlying political or allegorical purpose of its creation of a dystopian world achieves the utopian

function of offering the reader a radical alternative that reflects upon contemporary society."[6] Mathias Thaler has recently argued in a similar vein
and proposed the concept of melancholic hope as a contemporary utopian
mode that is rooted in a nuanced diagnosis of a disastrous present.[7]

This chapter starts from this connection between utopian and dystopian imagination and explores the antagonism of utopianism and philosophical pessimism. The aim will not be to return to the polemic and
reductive anti-utopian critiques of Cioran and Gray or to argue for either
one to be superior, more truthful or philosophically more accurate or rigorous than the other. Rather, I want to trace the seemingly counterintuitive dialectic of utopianism and pessimism. The central question is what
could be productive about engaging with what Eugene Thacker has called
the "nightside of thought"?[8] As Thacker has put it,

> [p]essimism is the lowest form of philosophy, frequently disparaged and
> dismissed, merely the symptom of a bad attitude. No one ever needs pessi-
> mism, in the way that one needs optimism to inspire one to great heights
> and to pick oneself up [...]. No one needs pessimism, and yet everyone—
> without exception—has, at some point in their lives, had to confront pessi-
> mism, if not as a philosophy, then as a grievance—against one's self or
> others, against one's surroundings or one's life, against the state of things or
> the world in general.[9]

How can this philosophy as grievance be of any help in rethinking utopianism? Both pessimism and utopianism are integral to prefigurative thought,
politics and aesthetics. While utopianism challenges what John Storey has
called "impossibilism",[10] for pessimism, "the world is brimming with negative possibility".[11] In the previous chapter, I have traced the dialectic of
the pessimism of the intellect and the optimism of the will in the thought
of the Frankfurt School thinkers Max Horkheimer and Theodor Adorno,
and in Stuart Hall's Gramscian theory of hegemony and conjunctural
analysis. In the present chapter, I want to expand on this notion by linking
different forms of pessimism to corresponding notions of utopianism to
see how the current trends of new pessimisms outlined in the introduction
to this book, address questions of utopianism.

In recent writing on utopianism, the strategy of defamiliarisation has
come to the fore of theorising the potential of utopianism to inspire and
articulate the desire for positive change and progress. Both Mathias Thaler
and John Storey have approached utopianism from this angle to challenge

a common criticism levelled at utopianists, namely that the utopian imagination is ill-equipped to face the harsh political and material realities of the world and is ultimately merely just that: a futile act of the imagination. Conversely, Thaler and Storey have argued that what utopianism can achieve is a defamiliarisation or derealisation of the present that challenges hegemonic notions of what is considered to be "realistic". Realism as an ideological mode is thus seen as the effect of an epistemological process that limits human thinking of what is deemed to be within the scope of the possible. This "impossibilism" is the hegemonic way of defining what "reality" is and what is possible and impossible within the limits of that "reality".[12] The concept of impossibilism thus emphasises the fact that being realistic is not merely a mode of perceiving the world as it really is but an epistemological and ideological disposition which renders some things thinkable and others unthinkable. Radical utopianism is an intervention into the preconditions of the thinkable and offers ways to consider new possibilities or at least to reframe the present. If, as A. Radhakrishnan and Eugene Thacker have argued, pessimism is likewise an epistemological disposition, then utopianism and pessimism can be seen as two different and sometimes even complimentary epistemological frames.[13] Throughout modern thought, pessimist thinkers have perceived utopianism as a provocation and have taken to task its various representatives. After all, as Eugene Thacker has sarcastically remarked, "[t]here is no better occasion for pessimism than optimism".[14] In many ways then, pessimism hinges on the struggle with utopia. If, as Joshua Foa Dienstag has argued, pessimism is the "hidden twin" of progress,[15] then it is no wonder that pessimism should have a close relationship with utopianism. This relationship, however, cannot merely be described as a straightforwardly antagonistic one.

It is worth going back to one of the most prominent representatives of modern pessimist thought, E. M. Cioran, to more fully understand the relationship between utopianism and pessimism. Cioran's critique of the utopian literary imagination and his philosophy of history, while scathingly polemic, offers opportunities to productively rethink this connection. This relationship has become more important in recent years, not only in the context of re-evaluations of utopianism such as Storey's and Thaler's. It is also a central element in the thought of contemporary pessimistic theorists such as John Gray, whose work is based on a rigorous critique of the modern idea of progress and utopianism. While Gray deconstructs the notion of (historical) progress and claims that utopian thinking, like religious fanaticism, can be potentially dangerous, Storey (who is indebted to the Gramscianism of Birmingham School theorists) holds a more optimistic view on utopianism as a mode of a radically progressive and emancipatory politics. The tension between utopianism and pessimism can also be seen in current strands of afrofuturist and afropessimist thought. After juxtaposing Cioran's critique of utopianism with Storey's idea of radical utopianism, I will engage with an example for this type of dialectic by analysing an episode from Steve McQueen's film anthology series *Small Axe* (2020), titled "Education", by interpreting it with the frameworks of afropessimism and "Black Utopia".[16] The analysis will illustrate the dialectic relationship of afropessimism with notions of (Black) utopia.

Utopianism Versus Pessimism

In his essay "Mechanism of Utopia", Cioran engages with the major works of utopian literature and offers a critique of the utopian imagination. His criticism of utopianism is based on aesthetic, moral and historical aspects and in particular takes aim at the representation of human nature and the philosophies of history and time underlying the utopian imagination, with paradise and apocalypse as the two potential directions of human history. The core of the utopian imagination is its teleological conception that conceives of human history as leading to the realisation of a better world. For Cioran, peaceful human coexistence is already unlikely—an improbability which nonetheless is a reality. Humanity's "mediocrity" and "impotence"[17] when it comes to fully act out the pervasive hatred of each against each, thus inadvertently leads to an unlikely and quasi-utopian situation. Considering humanity's flawed character which cannot even handle the basest emotions of animosity, it should be surprising, Cioran argues, that some humans can muster the imaginative ambition to think alternative and better societies. At the same time, however, Cioran concedes that utopian thinking is a pre-requisite of human community: "For we act only under the fascination of the impossible: which is to say that a society incapable of generating—and of dedicating itself to—utopia is threatened with sclerosis and collapse."[18] The problem that Cioran sees with the classical utopian imagination is that once the utopian longing for a better future eclipses the present in favour of a false teleological narrative, one is once more trapped in the promises of modern ideas of time and progress.

Thus, Cioran's polemic against utopias must be considered in the context of his thoughts on temporality and being. Elsewhere, he writes that "past, present, and future are merely variable appearances of one and the same disease [...]. And this disease is coextensive with Being".[19] The notion of a utopian telos thus must be rejected when one is "turning a cold shoulder to time".[20] Cioran's critique of utopia is thus connected to his philosophy of time and history. Cioran approaches utopian conceptions of time by asking, "Is it easier to confect a utopia than an apocalypse"?[21] Utopias, according to Cioran, have taken the place of Christianity in constructing a sense of telos: "Thus was born the Future, vision of an irrevocable happiness [...]."[22] What the monotheistic world religions with their ideas of apocalypse and paradise at the end of time have in common with utopias is a reversed sense of "nostalgia": "a nostalgia reversed, falsified, and vitiated, straining toward the future, obnubilated by 'progress', a temporal rejoinder, a jeering metamorphosis of the original paradise. [...]. Willy-nilly we bet on the future, make it into a panacea, and identifying it with the appearance of an altogether *different time* within time, we consider it as an inexhaustible and yet completed duration, a *timeless history*."[23] This is where utopias collide with actual history.

In consequence, this leads to Cioran's critique of "progress", which once again links utopias to Biblical ideas of the ideal place: "When Christ promised that the 'kingdom of God' was neither 'here' nor 'there', but within us, he doomed in advance the utopian constructions for which any 'kingdom' is necessarily *exterior*, with no relation to our inmost self or our individual salvation. So deeply have utopias marked us, that it is from outside, from the course of events or from the progress of collectivities that we await our deliverance. Thus was devised the Meaning of history, whose vogue would supplant that of Progress, without adding anything new to it. [...]. That history just unfolds, independently of a specified direction, of a goal, no one is willing to admit."[24] This is the crucial point of Cioran's pessimistic critique of utopias: they suffer from the same teleological understanding of time as the world religions. Instead of this, Cioran emphasises imperfection, accident, arbitrariness, meaninglessness and purposelessness.

While for Cioran every progressive effort is ultimately futile in the face of inevitable decay (everything and everyone will turn to dust, so why bother building a better world), John Storey argues that it is always paramount to desire a better world to gradually improve living conditions for future generations. Cioran might reject the idea of progress, yet he cannot help but be empathetic about the plight of the poor and their desires. This is where Cioran sees the "merits" of utopia: in their unabashed critique of poverty, driven by the "force of negation" of the present status quo.[25] This "force of negation", I would argue, bears similarities with Storey's concept of "defamiliarization". Cioran concludes his essay by addressing communism and anticommunism and the status of ideology in general. Writing in the late 1950s, Cioran seems in favour of the ideals by which communism is driven, but he also fears the negative effects of a totalising system of beliefs once it becomes the way of running things. What Cioran begrudgingly appreciates about the ideals of Marxism and communism is their sense of human compassion. Interestingly, he here offers a deconstruction (very much in a similar vein as Storey's defamiliarisation, but to different ends) of notions of reality: "Considered in itself, communism appears as the only reality to which one might still subscribe, if one harbors even a wisp of illusion as to the future."[26] However, he comes to the conclusion that communism would amount to the imposition of utopian illusion—an "*obligatory* optimism".[27]

An "obligatory optimism", for Cioran, is unacceptable—it is optimism for a better future turned into an imperative, an ideology. This is the unlikely place where Storey and Cioran meet: in their aim to deconstruct notions of reality and the (im)possible. Yet, while Storey remains a political optimist, Cioran, in the face of totalitarian communism in post-war Europe, deconstructs the becoming-ideological of utopian communism. Echoing Theodor Adorno's critique of "hurrah-optimism",[28] he intellectually fights for his right to be pessimistic rather than succumbing to "obligatory optimism". While Storey argues for the importance of hope as a driving force of positive change, Cioran considers hope a potentially dangerous force which not only delays the confrontation with the present in favour of focussing attention on a tomorrow that "is always imaginary".[29] He concludes his deconstruction of the utopian imagination by anticipating the mixing of utopia and apocalypse. While early utopian literature challenged the religious worldview of the Middle Ages and their ideas of Hell and apocalypse, Cioran's present of the twentieth century, with the experience of fascism, the World Wars and the emergence of Eastern Europe's communist dictatorships, sees "a contamination of utopia with apocalypse".[30] What transpires here in Cioran's conclusion is what could be called a pessimist utopianism. Cioran started his essay with what seemed to be an outright condemnation of all utopian literature, and he certainly proceeds in an unsparing and rigorous criticism of utopianism.

And yet, at the end of the essay, one cannot help but recognise in Cioran a hint of admiration for the ambition of the utopian imagination. This admiration transpires despite his sarcastic conclusion that in the face of the global political developments at the time of his writing—a post-World War Europe still in the grips of the Cold War giving lie to the ideological promises of the nineteenth and early twentieth centuries—both the religious and the secular variants of teleological narratives of salvation have collapsed. In a way, Cioran's notion of a utopia contaminated with apocalypse anticipates the contemporary trend of dystopian fiction.[31]

For Mathias Thaler, dystopian imagination can be the expression of a "melancholic hope" by acknowledging the disastrous potential of the present and the need to counterbalance it with a utopian impulse.[32] Thaler offers a critical reading of Colson Whitehead's novel *The Underground Railroad* as a "critical dystopia"—a term he takes from scholars of utopianism like Raffaella Baccolini, Gregory Claeys and Tom Moylan.[33] Critical dystopias "pivot around a type of hope that remains sensitive to the catastrophic failures of the past and alert to the immense perils of the present, without, however, foreclosing the prospect of a less violent, and less unequal future".[34] It seems, then, that in the current conjuncture of the progressing twenty-first century, utopianism has incorporated many of the criticism levelled at the utopian imagination by Cioran and others. Thus, John Storey's radical utopianism, which sets out to challenge our notions of reality—or "our dominant constructions of reality and our complicity with them",[35] can also be considered as a contemporary, more nuanced approach to utopianism. Storey argues that the naturalisation of a certain sense of reality dictates what we consider possible and what is supposed to be impossible. We are all complicit in this construction of reality because we perpetuate the belief that certain alternatives are just not possible. This "impossibilism" is an epistemological angle that Storey wants to challenge and disrupt with the mode of utopianism as a form of what he calls "derealisation".[36]

Storey historicises the (im)possible. He looks at how human desire for change and for a better world is historically contingent. He does the same with the notion of human nature. Storey challenges the critique of utopian texts which are based on the claim that utopias do not take into consideration the complexities and flaws of human nature. Could "impossibilism" just be another word for pessimism? To some degree, it is pessimistic because it pre-emptively declares possibilities unfeasible. However, it is far from a substantial philosophical pessimism. After all, as I have shown in the second chapter, philosophical pessimism can amount to a critique of reality or realism that, as I want to show in this chapter, is on a par with the derealisation of radical utopianism.

If radical utopianism in its double articulation intends to raise expectations, then pessimism—perhaps quite obviously—wants to lower expectations. Storey challenges the critique of utopian texts which are based on the claim that utopias do not take into consideration the complexities and flaws of human nature. This is something that Cioran also does in his essay. Cioran of course has a deeply pessimistic and misanthropic outlook on humanity which he argues contradicts the aims of most utopias. Without mentioning Cioran, Storey argues that human nature is not something static and unchanging, to begin with:

> The idea that replacing 'real people' is what utopia is really about is not only a simplification of human nature, it is a simplification of the history of utopianism. It assumes that human nature and human history are completed projects—real people exist in the real world, supposedly at the end of human history. It is only if we abandon the movement of history that we arrive at such a fixed idea of human nature.[37]

So, human nature does seem to change and is a part of historical developments as much as everything else. It is, as Storey says, in "a state of becoming".[38] This fundamentally informs the optimism expressed in his book. Of course, such a view of humanity's potential for change can be challenged from a perspective informed by philosophical pessimism, whether it is a metaphysical pessimism or the ethical pessimism of Critical Theory.

From such a perspective, it does not matter much in the grand scheme of things. As Adorno and Horkheimer observe in their conversation on utopia: "In the long run things cannot change. The possibility of regression is always there [...]. Relapse into barbarism is always an option."[39] Like Cioran, Adorno and Horkheimer refuse to see human progress as a linear, teleological process: as Horkheimer observes, "[e]very new generation has to become civilized all over again".[40] However, Adorno and Horkheimer are not content with stopping their argument at this ethically pessimist conclusion. There is a hint of Storey's notion of derealisation of "impossibilism" when they point out that the utopian "possibility of a completely unshackled reality remains valid".[41] Thus, like Storey, Adorno and Horkheimer attempt to historicise the (im)possible. However, they do so in the full awareness of potential catastrophe. Theirs is a critical utopianism which is based on a pessimist analysis of the historical conditions of change.

AFROFUTURISM AND AFROPESSIMISM

Juxtaposing afrofuturism and afropessimism demonstrates the complexities of contemporary conceptions of the future in the face of catastrophe. While afropessimism sees the present and future of Black lives as caught in permanent transhistorical social death, afrofuturism works through this historical trauma and uses it as the precondition for imagining the future otherwise. It is utopian in Cioran's sense in that it is fully aware of the apocalypse. For afrofuturists, the apocalypse diagnosed by afropessimists has already happened and continues to happen every day in the present. And yet, from this apocalypse, a different future can emerge. An example of afrofuturism that is illustrative of this is John Akomfrah's documentary essay film *The Last Angel of History* (1996). Akomfrah's film takes its departure from ruins in the present: the industrial ruins of Detroit, the ruins of human history, the ruins of an exploited continent. It takes the notion of crossroads from Robert Johnson's blues song in which he details how he met the devil at the crossroads and sold his soul in exchange for the blues. In Akomfrah's film, the crossroads becomes the site of an archaeological dig which opens up the pathways of the past and the future. *The Last Angel of History* is acutely aware of the traumatic history of slavery and genocide. That it embraces notions of afrofuturism does not mean that it denies this history—on the contrary: the utopian futures of afrofuturism are generated from the historical trauma of African colonisation. Afrofuturism is simultaneously looking backward and forward, as Daniel Kojo Schrade explains: "Afrofuturism immediately has to do with research, bringing the future and the past together, while activating the space in-between. [...]. Looking backwards while imagining oneself in the future and being aware of the space in-between requires a lot of discipline."[42] Afrofuturism is thus indebted to a genuinely modern understanding of what Eva Horn has described as *"the future as a garden of forking paths"*, a "contingent future subject to change",[43] and thus rejects a dominant historical telos. Rather, as Kodwo Eshun explains in *The Last Angel of History*, Africa can be rendered as "a lost continent of the past" as well as "an alien future".[44] The titular reference to Walter Benjamin's image of the Angel of History, who simultaneously faces the debris of a catastrophic past while about to be caught in the storm of future progress[45] figures this notion of a contingent future. This contingency is also embodied in Akomfrah's film in the legend of blues musician Robert Johnson meeting the Devil at the crossroads. Akomfrah's film takes this image of the crossroads further and makes it a site of archaeology of African cultural pasts that can pave the way for its futures. As the film's narratorial Data Thief—a figure who "haunts the present from the future"[46]—explains: "If you can make an archaeological dig into this crossroads, you can find fragments, techno fossils ... and if you can put those fragments together, you have a code ... crack that code, and you have a key to the future."[47]

Such an archaeology—akin to Fredric Jameson's notion of an archaeology of the future[48]—however, must always face the challenge of reconciling the traumatic pasts of African peoples with their potentially utopian futures. Alex Zamalin's recent argument about "Black Utopia" is a case in point. Zamalin argues that Black American utopianism has not been sufficiently acknowledged by scholars because "black American life has been nothing short of dystopian".[49] Black utopians and anti-utopians, Zamalin argues, are united by their examination of the "hidden dynamics and logical consequences of racism".[50] Zamalin emphasises that utopianism, especially in the context of Black futurity, should not be equated with an uncritical faith in progress. In fact, he argues for a Black utopianism that is coupled with an anti-utopianism that critically intervenes in the narratives of continuous social and economic progress espoused by mainstream politics, including its representatives of the contemporary left.[51] Zamalin's approach echoes the dialectic of pessimist critique and utopian imagination in Adorno and Horkheimer. Zamalin also addresses critics of utopianism who blame it for its alleged unreflected attitude towards ideals of linear progress.[52] It is in fact the mode of critique that he identifies as a vital integral component of proper utopianism.

While Black utopianism and afrofuturism imagine Black futures in the full awareness of and a response to the traumatic histories of colonialism, slavery and present-day racism and thus use prefigurative imaginaries as a tool of resistance, afropessimism opts for an altogether different approach. If, as Daniel Kojo Schrade states, it requires discipline to imagine oneself in the future while facing one's past, this is especially due to the fact that "African peoples have been forcibly restricted from access to our histories".[53] Rather than offering ways of digging the archive to produce future imaginaries, contemporary afropessimism presents itself as a disruptive "metatheory"[54] that radically challenges theories of liberation, whether they emerge from postcolonial, antiracist, Marxist or feminist theories, activism and struggles. Like thinkers that align themselves with afrofuturist projects, afropessimist thinkers grapple with the temporalities affected by the history of colonialism and slavery and the resulting experience of suffering. However, they come to different conclusions. As Frank B. Wilderson III argues, "Black suffering" is "a suffering without a solution", a "suffering that fuels the psychic health of the rest of the world".[55] Thinking as an afropessimist thus means recognising the fact that the existence of Black bodies constitutes "the foil of Humanity".[56] Like other current afropessimists, Wilderson is indebted to Orlando Patterson's notion of "social death"—an ontological condition that results from the history of slavery and its denial of Black subject- and personhood.[57] This condition of social death constitutes a "meta-aporia"[58]: "no Blacks are in the world, but, by the same token, there is no world without Blacks".[59]

Wilderson recounts a conversation with his mother who, as a supporter of Martin Luther King and Barack Obama and appalled by her son's rejection of electoral politics, asks about the practical use of afropessimism. Wilderson argues that people are "too afraid" of afropessimism because they are "[a]fraid of a problem in which everyone is complicit and for which no sentence can be written that would explain how to remedy it".[60] What afropessimism shares with other forms of pessimism, then, is its deliberate refusal to be particularly useful or constructive. And yet, its purpose might rest in the fact that it articulates (and thus offers Black people the freedom to articulate) the otherwise unsayable about social relations in cultures marked by white hegemony. The political and intellectual conflict with his mother, a believer in political progress and the potential of the United States to achieve a post-racist society, is representative of the political potential of pessimist thought outlined by Joshua Foa Dienstag:

> pessimism attacks the roots of modern political orders by denying their sense of time. [...]. In suggesting that we look at time and history differently, it asks us to alter radically our opinion both of ourselves and what we can expect from politics. It does not simply tell us to expect less. It tells us, in fact, to expect nothing.[61]

Wilderson's sarcastic refusal to believe in the political promises of the Obama era is representative of this pessimistic stance on politics and notions of progress. This refusal to put faith in the temporality of political change is, as R. Radhakrishnan has shown, an epistemological "act of will" with which the afropessimist rejects dominant narratives of historical progress.[62]

Wilderson's afropessimism thus becomes a countermodel to more optimistic and possibly even utopian visions of Black futurity. If, for instance, juxtaposed with Anna Everett's description of "Trump-Time", the afropessimist intervention into temporality can be demonstrated. For Everett, Trump-Time "signifies a delimited temporal precarity that suggests, if not predicts, a short-lived or ruptured period of time and influence. The hope or idea here is that black people will endure Trump-Time as a temporary and pessimistic existential moment haunted by that seemingly more optimistic memory of black futurity promised by the hopeful, if not giddy, Obama Era".[63] Everett tries to reconcile what she describes as the seeming contrast between today's afrofuturism and the "black trauma and terror" during the Trump years.[64] The challenge, for Everett, is to "reconcile my strangely enjoyable post-Obama nostalgia disrupted completely with the very real existential dangers of Trump-Time to visible black bodies like my own".[65] What is at stake from this perspective, then, is the failure or waning of the utopian promise of the eight years of America's first Black president. Trump-Time thus constitutes a crisis in utopian and afrofuturist temporality. For an afropessimist like Wilderson, however, a nostalgic longing for the utopian promise of the Obama years would be an impossibility since the temporality of electoral and state politics still operates in the service of a notion of the Human that relies on the unbeing and social death of Black bodies. Perceived afropessimistically, "Trump-Time" is no diversion from (and therefore not a crisis of) a regular temporality of American politics, but its logical continuation. In other words, if afropessimism can be reconciled at all with notions of Black utopia and afrofuturism, then these must emerge from their own sense of temporality and must never operate according to the temporal parameters of US-American politics.

Thus, Wilderson's afropessimism is an intervention into dominant historical narratives of alleged post-racial and inclusive progress. Remembering his youth, Wilderson observes his experience with temporality: "As a boy I seldom lived in the present. It hurt too much to be in the present. When I occurred to myself I was myself in the future. The present was my penance, what I had to pay for my soot. I dreamed that the present would pass one day."[66] However, he realises as a boy that he cannot escape the temporality he is trapped in via his Black body: "I knew [...] that the present would always be waiting for me".[67] This realisation of presentism not only questions dominant notions of political progress (the more time passes since the formal end of slavery, the more equal Black people will be in

American society) but also precludes any kind of Black utopianism and afrofuturism (how can one see oneself in the future when one is already dead in the present?). In many ways, Wilderson's becoming-afropessimist gestures towards confronting the obstructive and paralysing present that he feels as a boy. The episodes of mental illness in his later adult life described throughout the book thus can be interpreted as symptomatic of the sense of a perpetual being trapped in history. In this context, afropessimism, much like psychoanalysis, becomes painful working through a state of grief, a state of being stuck in time.

Although a full reconciliation of afropessimist and utopian perspectives might be difficult, it can nevertheless be resolved in a dialectic relationship that proves to be productive for critical readings of contemporary cultural texts. British director Steve McQueen's film anthology series *Small Axe* proves to be such a text that is representative of the current conjuncture. Broadcast by the BBC in 2020, *Small Axe* was hailed as a celebration of the history and identity of the West-Indian diaspora in Britain. Each film in the anthology is a self-contained story of the lives of West Indian immigrants in London in the 1960s–80s, often drawing on historical events. I want to engage with the series as an opportunity to explore the possibility of a pessimist-utopian dialectic in the wider context of the debates on afropessimism, Black utopia and afrofuturism. I take my cue from several comments in the debate on the anthology, including those of its director, Steve McQueen. While the individual films are largely indebted to the narrative conventions of historical films, biopics and the aesthetics of British social realism, McQueen himself considers them as Black "science fiction pictures": "These films are all about the future because they tell us where we're at, how far we've come, and where we need to go."[68] In a similar vein, film scholar Clive James Nwonka has commented on the anthology that its forceful representation of Black British culture and history constitutes a "unique cultural event"—an event, however, that despite its celebratory character also comes with a "sense of impending loss, longing, and [...] a number of utopian questions".[69] Among these utopian questions are questions about representation, history and time. Will there ever be a time when a series like *SmallAxe* will be a "non-event"?[70] Or will the British film and television industry resort to the normal, read predominantly white, state of affairs? As an intervention into representational media regimes, British historiography and cultural memory, *Small Axe*'s utopian potential must inevitably come with a profound sense of Black melancholia—a grieving for the future akin to Wilderson's inability to see himself in the future. It is in the context of this double bind that the episode "Education" can be read with the dialectic of afropessimism and Black utopianism.

In the final film of the series, 12-year-old Kingsley struggles to keep up in school. He is obsessed with physics and astronomy and dreams of becoming an astronaut, but is hindered by his dyslexia. Impatient white teachers convince his parents that it is best to send him to a "School for the Educationally Subnormal". Distracted by their demanding work lives, Kingsley's parents are unaware that the structurally dysfunctional school is inadequate for their son's education and is marred by dysfunctional structures and poorly trained teachers. Kingsley's mental health deteriorates and it becomes clear that the school renders its pupils, who are predominantly from the lower classes and of minority-ethnic background, into a position of social death. While the school is by no means exclusively tending to Black children, with its pupils coming from diverse structurally disadvantaged backgrounds, it is clear that the criteria for who has "special needs" are racially biased. This structural disadvantage is internalised by many of the Black characters in the film. Nina, one of Kingsley's fellow students, denies the fact that she is Black in a conversation with the school psychologist Hazel, who tells her that she is proud to be Black. When asked about what they learn about the history of their ancestors, the Black children answer that their history lessons teach them "that we were slaves", effectively fixing Black life in Britain in the ontological framework of perpetual colonialism.[71]

Later, during a meeting of Black activists who want to help parents to get their Black children out of special needs schools, one mother admits to hating her own children for bringing home the traces of the school system and "this whole blasted country system"—a country which she came to with a dream for her family's future. Now, she says, her children remind her that she has "no dream to pass on."[72] Here, afropessimism in the British postimperial context becomes the mood of what Sara Ahmed has labelled the "melancholic migrant".[73] This mother's painful admission of projecting her hate and disappointment in the promise of migration onto her own children speaks to a broken sense of time and lost future. If "culture becomes what unfolds over time",[74] then the migrant's realisation that one's hope for future happiness clashes with the inherent racism of British culture produces a sense of being stuck in time. Similarly, Kingsley's dreams for the future—prefigured in the film's first images of space as seen by Kingsley during a visit to the planetarium, are being stalled by his miseducation. Time does not progress—or rather, one realises that a nation's time—the time of Empire—and one's own time do not align. The Black mother's hate and pessimism are the feelings of the "melancholic migrant"—a figure "who refuses to participate in the national game"[75] and becomes an "affect alien" that is "out of line with the public mood."[76]

Rather than working and living towards his anticipated future, the "special needs" school constitutes a space outside of lived time. "Black life", Jared Sexton argues about social death, "is not lived in the world that the world lives in, but underground, in outer space".[77] Thus, according to the afropessimist argument, the afterlife of slavery produces its unique temporality that diverges from the temporality of the world of the (white) Human. The film captures this experience of temporality in long scenes conveying Kingsley's boredom during lessons, and his attempt to manage his frustration and escape the pressures of everyday life by submerging himself in water in the bathtub—like the young Frank B. Wilderson, he is in search of a sensual experience able to transport him out of the temporality of an eternal present. "Education" repeatedly demonstrates McQueen's directorial interest in the problem of passing time. Throughout the film, McQueen captures the excruciating boredom and resulting absurdity of the lessons at the special needs school. The camera lingers on the children's apathetic faces as they struggle not to fall asleep while their teacher indulges himself with his acoustic guitar. Boredom, as Joshua Foa Dienstag has argued, is not only a uniquely human condition but also one of the prime concerns of pessimist thinkers. As a "marker for time-boundedness", boredom is the result of human awareness of one's own historicity and the absurdity of the notion of historical progress—a "disenchanted universe offers us nothing else".[78] In "Education", boredom exposes not only the absurdity of history and temporality per se but also the absurdity of human institutions that are used to separate and classify human beings into "normal" and "subnormal". Even worse, the time experienced in the special needs school is not only the time of boredom, but the time of detention and social death. Black being has been rendered abject. If McQueen's film is read at least partly as a pessimist film in that it provides a pessimistic mode of analysis of a sociohistorical moment, then the film's pessimism consists in exposing different experiences of temporalities. Temporalities, in this case, are not a neutral fact but are experienced in the modes of race and class.

But the film contrasts this bleak situation with utopian potential. If, as Carl A. Grant has proposed, afropessimism can be used as a lens and framework for progressive Black education and to foster "radical hope",[79] then a version of this can be found in the film's grassroots initiative of West Indian women working in education who provide legal counselling for the parents of children rendered "educationally subnormal". The grassroots initiative offers alternative supplementary Saturday schools for Black children, teaching them the African history of their ancestors that is being ignored or distorted in the British school system in an informal Black History Discussion Group. The private lessons empower the Black kids who were led to believe by their schools that their history begins with slavery. Kingsley overcomes his dyslexia and is sent back to regular school. If, as director McQueen has stated, his anthology might be read as science fiction, then this can be seen in the framing of "Education". The film begins and ends with an image of space while Kingsley reads a text about Africa's ancient history, suggestive of a utopian vision of the future born from the restored past.

The notion of education is central to the nexus of pessimist diagnosis and utopian possibility. The film explores education as both a tool of power and exclusion and as a means for empowerment and utopian resistance. The Black children and teenagers failed by the British school system are encouraged to engage with the past as a way to rewrite their history and their future. Pessimism asks us to "rethink our sense of time" and to "challenge our notions of order and meaning".[80] The rethinking of historiography and the educational apparatus in McQueen's short film works in a similar vein. Pessimism and utopianism become tools for disrupting educational institutions and their hegemonic sense of history and progress. They offer new epistemologies that include minoritarian perspectives and through rewriting history open up the horizon of expectations towards the future.

The grassroots initiative and their empowerment through education restore a sense of the West-Indian community's own temporality, their past and their future to overcome stuckness in the present. In doing so, they not only challenge the hegemonic temporality of British institutions and the state—they also practice counterhegemonic forms of care which constitute utopian practices. Rather than putting false hopes and optimism—which can only ever be a "cruel" or "obligatory" optimism[81]—into white institutions, their pessimist diagnosis identifies these institutions as careless institutions when it comes to the lives of Black people in Britain. In the context of McQueen's film, (afro)pessimism becomes a mode of critique which abandons false and harmful hopes in the institutions from a minoritarian perspective. This echoes the diagnosis of the neoliberal dismantling of the caring state formulated by the Care Collective in their *Care Manifesto*. Rather than subscribing to the myth of "self-discipline",[82] the Black utopianism in "Education" consists in a new radical relational politics. Shona Hunter identifies those everyday practices as "relational politics" which offer the potential for renewal within the structures of the dysfunctional state and its institutions. Rather than abandoning the uncaring state altogether, then, relational politics consists of those forms of agency which manifest despite the institutions' "managerial desocialization".[83] In that respect, it is important to note that the grassroots initiative in McQueen's film is run exclusively by Black women. It is thus radical Black feminist politics that shape and drive this utopian response to the "social system of *organized loneliness*".[84] The real-life grassroots movement that the film reconstructs thus shares similarities with the twenty-first-century demands of the Care Collective which promotes feminist queer and marginalised forms of kinship and solidarity as models for a future system of care.

Pessimist-Utopian Care?

As the discussion of afropessimism and Black utopia has shown, the tension between utopianism and pessimism continues to be a central factor of contemporary modes of prefiguration. Their relationship, however, is not the one of straightforward antagonism that the polemic pessimist criticism of utopian thought by thinkers like E. M. Cioran and John Gray might suggest. Rather, as the relationship of afropessimism and Black utopia suggests, pessimism is in a continuous dialogue with utopianism that amounts to a more complex dialectic relationship. If we accept Joshua Foa Dienstag's assessment, echoed by Frank B. Wilderson's afropessimism, that pessimism's intervention in modern political thought suggests that we should expect nothing, then this is not an inevitable condemnation of passivity. Rather, pessimism's rejection of progressivist narratives and obligatory/cruel optimism can open a new horizon of expectation. Not unlike Storey's radical utopianism, such a kind of pessimism rejects hegemonic framings of what progress can mean. So how can one care for the future from a position of pessimism? The (afro)pessimist-utopian reading of Steve McQueen's film "Education" shows that reclaiming one's cultural history can begin with a pessimist diagnosis which is necessary to prefigure a different future that radically questions existing institutions.

What if our own attachment to institutions of care have become cruelly optimistic while we are standing in the ruins of the present? When faced with this kind of cruel optimism, an optimism that cruelly tells us to just passively indulge in the false "excitement at the prospect of 'the change that's gonna come'",[85] a pessimist mode of critique might be liberating.

As Shona Hunter, argues, false optimism in dysfunctional institutions can be substituted with what she calls "melancholic hope":

> Hope is not a matter of optimism as such, but a matter of more agonistic relational practice which is only achievable within the context of difference, disagreement and uncertainty over the nature of reality. [...] hope sits in the contested space between a knowable and achievable shared reality and a projection of something else that might be, where that something else cannot be known either in advance or retrospectively, it can only be playfully fantasised about and tested out through practice in the present.[86]

A pessimism of theory can work as a means to dismantle the unhealthy attachment to notions of care. What is more, if coupled with an optimism of the will and of praxis, one might even arrive at new utopian visions for the future of care. Pessimism, as a reflective mode, then, can become an analytical tool to assess the demise of social institutions, but it can also sever the cruelly optimistic binds with which we cling to the fantasy of the caring institution and the caring state. Getting rid of this fantasy might pave the way for new modes of collective solidarity and a new ethics of care.

NOTES

1. Cf. E. M. Cioran, *History and Utopia* (New York: Arcade, 2015); John Gray, *Straw Dogs: Thoughts on Humans and Other Animals* (London: Granta, 2003); John Gray, *Black Mass: Apocalyptic Religion and the Death of Utopia* (Penguin, 2008); John Gray, *The Silence of Animals: On Progress and Other Modern Myths* (London: Penguin, 2014).
2. Caroline Edwards, *Utopia and the Contemporary British Novel* (Cambridge: Cambridge University Press, 2019), p. 18.
3. John Gray, *Black Mass: Apocalyptic Religion and the Death of Utopia* (London: Penguin, 2008).
4. Cf. Erik Olin Wright, *Envisioning Real Utopias* (London: Verso, 2010); Ruth Levitas, *Utopia as Method: The Imaginary Reconstitution of Society* (Houndsmills: Palgrave, 2013); Davina Cooper, *Everyday Utopias: The Conceptual Life of Promising Spaces* (Durham: Duke University Press, 2013).

5. Edwards 2019, p. 39; Fredric Jameson, *Archaeologies of the Future. The Desire Called Utopia and Other Science Fictions* (London: Verso, 2005), p. xvi.
6. Edwards, 2019, p. 42.
7. Mathias Thaler, "Bleak Dreams, Not Nightmares: Critical Dystopias and the Necessity of Melancholic Hope", *Constellations* 26, no. 4 (December 2019): 607–622.
8. Eugene Thacker, *Cosmic Pessimism* (Minneapolis: Univocal, 2015), p. 3.
9. Thacker, 2015, pp. 3–4.
10. John Storey, *Radical Utopianism and Cultural Studies: On Refusing to Be Realistic* (Abingdon: Routledge, 2019), p. 7.
11. Thacker, 2015, p. 9.
12. Storey, 2019, p. 7.
13. R. Radhakrishnan, "The Epistemology of Pessimism", *The Comparatist*, no. 43 (2019): 41–67, p. 42; Eugene Thacker, *Starry Speculative Corpse: Horror of Philosophy 2* (Winchester: Zero Books, 2015b), p. 138; see also the introduction in this book.
14. Thacker, 2018, p. 61.
15. Joshua Foa Dienstag, *Pessimism: Philosophy, Ethic, Spirit* (New Jersey: Princeton University Press, 2006), p. 16 and see also Introduction.
16. I use the term in reference to Alex Zamalin's book *Black Utopia: The History of an Idea from Black Nationalism to Afrofuturism* (New York: Columbia University Press, 2019).
17. Cioran, 2015, p. 80.
18. Cioran, 2015, p. 81.
19. E. M. Cioran, *A Short History of Decay* (London: Penguin, 2018), p. 55.
20. Cioran, 2018, p. 55; see also Dienstag's discussion of Cioran's critique of "modern optimism" and teleological faith in historical progress, cf. Dienstag, 2006, pp. 133–135
21. Cioran, 2015, p. 83.
22. Cioran, 2015, p. 89.
23. Cioran, 2015, pp. 88–89.
24. Cioran, 2015, p. 91.
25. Cioran, 2015, p. 82
26. Cioran, 2015, p. 96.
27. Cioran, 2015, p. 96.
28. Theodor Adorno, *Minima Moralia: Reflections from Damaged Life* (London: Verso, 2020), p. 122.
29. Dienstag, 2006, p. 135.
30. Cioran, 2015, pp. 97–98.
31. John Storey, *Consuming Utopia: Cultural Studies and the Politics of Reading* (Abingdon: Routledge, 2022), pp. 31–44.

32. Cf. Thaler, 2019.
33. Thaler, 2019, p. 608.
34. Thaler, 2019, p. 608.
35. Storey, 2019, p. 1.
36. Storey, 2019, p. 5.
37. Storey, 2019, p. 8.
38. Storey, 2019, p. 8.
39. Theodor Adorno and Max Horkheimer, *Towards a New Manifesto* (London: Verso, 2019), pp. 14–15.
40. Adorno and Horkheimer, 2019, p. 32.
41. Adorno and Horkheimer, 2019, p. 14.
42. Henriette Gunkel and Daniel Kojo Schrade, "Scavenging the Future of the Archive: A Conversation between Henriette Gunkel and Daniel Kojo Schrade", in *Futures & Fictions*, ed. Henriette Gunkel, Ayesha Hameed, and Simon O'Sullivan (London: Repeater, 2017), 193–211, p. 195.
43. Eva Horn, *The Future as Catastrophe: Imagining Disaster in the Modern Age* (New York: Columbia University Press, 2018), p. 190.
44. *The Last Angel of History,* directed by John Akomfrah (Black Audio Film Collective / ZDF, 1996).
45. Cf. Walter Benjamin, *Illuminations* (New York: Knopf, 1969), pp. 257–8. For an exploration of the importance of Walter Benjamin and Ernst Bloch's concept of utopian hope in John Akomfrah's work, see Annett Busch, "How Much the Heart Can Hold", in *Futures & Fictions*, ed. Simon O'Sullivan Henriette Gunkel, Ayesha Hameed (London: Repeater, 2017), 122–43.
46. Kara Keeling, *Queer Times, Black Futures* (New York: New York University Press, 2019), p. 126.
47. *The Last Angel of History,* 1996.
48. Jameson, 2005.
49. Zamalin, 2019, p. 6.
50. Zamalin, 2019, p. 11.
51. Cf. Zamalin, 2019, pp. 143–144.
52. Cf. Zamalin, 2019, pp. 138–139.
53. kara lynch and Henriette Gunkel, "Lift Off … An Introduction", in *We Travel the Space Ways: Black Imagination, Fragments, and Diffractions* (Bielefeld: Transcript, 2019), 21–43, p. 27.
54. Frank B. Wilderson III., *Afropessimism* (New York: Liveright, 2020), p. 14.
55. Wilderson III., 2020, p. 329.
56. Wilderson III., 2020, p. 13.
57. Wilderson III., 2020, p. 40.
58. Wilderson III., 2020, p. 13.
59. Wilderson III., 2020, p. 40.

60. Wilderson III., 2020, p. 328.
61. Dienstag, 2006, p. 5.
62. Radhakrishnan, 2019, p. 48.
63. Anna Everett, "Afrofuturism on My Mind: Imagining Black Lives in a Post-Obama World", in *We Travel the Space Ways: Black Imagination, Fragments, and Diffractions* (Bielefeld: Transcript, 2019), 251–78, p. 256.
64. Everett, 2019, p. 256.
65. Everett, 2019, p. 257.
66. Wilderson III, 2020, p. 21.
67. Wilderson III, 2020, p. 21.
68. McQueen qtd. in Keith Nelson Jr., 'The Unnatural Human Nature of Steve McQueen's "Small Axe"', *Complex*, 20 November 2020, https://www.complex.com/pop-culture/2020/11/steve-mcqueen-small-axe-anthology-interview
69. Clive James Nwonka, "Small Axe Has Become a Unique Cultural Event for Black Britain", *The Big Issue*, 13 December 2020, https://www.bigissue.com/opinion/small-axe-has-become-a-unique-cultural-event-for-black-britain/
70. Nwonka, 2020.
71. *Small Axe: Education*, directed by Steve McQueen (BBC Film, 2020).
72. *Small Axe*, 2020.
73. Sara Ahmed, *The Promise of Happiness* (Durham: Duke University Press, 2010), p. 121.
74. Ahmed, 2010, p. 159.
75. Ahmed, 2010, p. 142
76. Ahmed, 2010, p. 157.
77. Jared Sexton, "The Social Life of Social Death: On Afro-Pessimism and Black Optimism", in *Time, Temporality and Violence in International Relations: (De)Fatalizing the Present, Forging Radical Alternatives*, ed. Anna M. Agathangelou and Kyle D. Killian (Abingdon: Routledge, 2016), 61–75, p. 69.
78. Dienstag, 2006, p. 31.
79. Dienstag, 2006, p. 65.
80. Dienstag, 2006, p. 5.
81. Cf. Lauren Berlant, *Cruel Optimism* (Durham: Duke University Press, 2011); Cioran 2015, p. 96.
82. The Care Collective, *The Care Manifesto: The Politics of Interdependence* (London: Verso, 2020), p. 12.
83. Shona Hunter, *Power, Politics and the Emotions: Impossible Governance?* (Abingdon: Routledge, 2015), p. 12; 16–17.
84. The Care Collective, 2020, p. 45, emphasis in original.
85. Berlant, 2011, p. 2.
86. Hunter, 2015, p. 176.

CHAPTER 4

The Kids Will Not Be Alright: Grievable Futures and the Ethics of Reproductive Pessimism

Abstract Antinatalist philosophies and queer pessimism have been flourishing since the 2000s. Both are united by what can be called their reproductive pessimism. Reproductive pessimism critically interrogates the ethics of human reproduction and challenges dominant notions of temporality and futurity. This chapter will compare these pessimist critiques of "reproductive futurism" (Lee Edelman) and explore cultural texts that likewise challenge and disrupt the temporalities of reproductive futurism. Ted Chiang's novella "Story of Your Life", its film adaptation *Arrival* directed by Denis Villeneuve and Gaspar Noé's film *Irréversible* deconstruct linear conceptions of time in their radical experiments with the literary and cinematic narration of temporality. They do so to explore an ethical dilemma: If the future was knowable, would it be morally acceptable to create future human beings and thus sentient life? Is it possible to mourn the future if the future is only imaginable "as catastrophe" (Eva Horn)? And what cultural representational forms would be suitable to make the future "grievable"? Such experiments with time, the ethical implications of human procreation and futures to be mourned are the paradigmatic cultural form of contemporary pessimism.

Keywords Reproductive pessimism • Antinatalism • Queer pessimism • Mourning • Grief • Gaspar Noé • Ted Chiang • Denis Villeneuve • Sara Ahmed • David Benatar

© The Author(s), under exclusive license to Springer Nature Switzerland AG 2023
M. Schmitt, *Spectres of Pessimism*,
https://doi.org/10.1007/978-3-031-25351-5_4

The Child as Figuration of the Future

Can we mourn the future? This question seems to haunt contemporary imaginings of human futurity and has repercussions for how we think about the ethics of reproduction. In Paul Schrader's film *First Reformed* (2017), environmental activist Michael despairs at the prospect of being responsible for bringing a child into a world that he knows will collapse under the strain of multiple ecological crises. Seeing "the future as catastrophe",[1] he imagines his yet unborn child accusing him in the future of having brought them into this world despite his knowledge of the worst. Michael, about to become a father, affectively lives in the future and mourns the near-future effects of ecological destruction from the point of view of his future child, and thus, prefiguratively mourns the future his child should have but will not have. Schrader's film turns the prospect of a dying planet into a spiritual and theological problem—"can God forgive us for what we have done to His world?"—and leaves open the question of what this horizon of expectation entails for the ethics of reproduction.[2] *First Reformed* thus explores the conundrums of prefigurative thinking about posteriority and procreation that are symptomatic of the contemporary perception of an increasingly precarious present and near future.

In her reading of climate change novels and "the limits of parental care ethics", Adeline Johns-Putra formulates these challenges by asking, "what would happen if the future could talk back? What would be the point of view from a posterity in receipt of a parental ethics of care [...]?"[3] If the care for future generations is primarily focussed on the care for one's immediate genetic offspring, Johns-Putra argues, this narrowed focus risks limiting the view of the "unknowable future" to just the "knowable present", thus restricting an ethical position to decisions which "are based on the values and interests of the present" in the light of the "absence and powerlessness of future generations."[4] If understood in this way, a parental ethics of care focussed on one's own immediate lineage is compromised in that it excludes the nonhuman world and those groups and individuals that do not immediately genetically belong to one's lineage. What is more, a focus on the survival and well-being of one's own child might also risk being merely a replaced fulfilment of one's own narcissistic desires, which (if seen from a eudaemonic perspective) might culminate in a disregard for the actual needs of future generations. Johns-Putra here refers to Lee Edelman's polemic against a "reproductive futurism" which posits the figure of the Child as the sole focus of (heteronormative) concerns for future and posterity.[5] To continue Johns-Putra's argument, one would have to ask for cultural and narrative forms that can, to repurpose a concept central to Judith Butler's thought, make the future "grievable".[6]

This chapter will engage with the ethical questions that arise from this notion of future grievability by looking at fictional texts which address Johns-Putra's questions by developing scenarios in which the future actually does talk back. Ted Chiang's science fiction novella "Story of Your Life" (1998/2002) and Denis Villeneuve's film adaptation *Arrival* (2016) imagine an encounter with an alien species whose concepts of time and language are nonlinear, allowing them to experience past, present and future simultaneously, and likewise allowing them to communicate this simultaneity in their language. I want to centre the story's engagement with the narrator-protagonist's reflection of temporality and futurity and her decision to have a child from the perspective of a pessimist ethics of futurity. I will contrast this with Gaspar Noé's experiment in cinematic backwards narration, the controversial rape-revenge drama *Irréversible* (2002), whose apodictic motto "le temps détruit tout" (time destroys all things) suggests a pessimist theory of time which begs the question of how to make ethical decisions about procreation in the light of the inevitable futurity of destruction and decay. Such fictional experiments with reverse and nonlinear narration are particularly suited to explore the ethical questions of procreation from both optimistic and pessimistic angles. These fictional scenarios offer ways to engage with the reproductive pessimism that unites queer pessimism and antinatalism.

From Reproductive Futurism to Reproductive Pessimism

The capacity for envisioning good or even happy futures requires the ability to have hope and to trust in time as being on your side. This can entail being hopeful for one's own happiness in the future, or believing in positive possibilities for loved ones, one's community or for the human species. Hope and faith in the future are more often than not anthropocentric, or species-centred. Being hopeful about the future is connected to the ability to see one's own life as meaningful for the present as well as for the future. It is not surprising, then, that the figure of the Child is often considered as the embodiment of hopeful futures as well as of a meaningful life. Procreation thus can become a default criterion for measuring a meaningful life. Not surprisingly, the child becomes a central figuration of meaningful and hopeful futures in narrative. Queer and feminist theorists such as Lee Edelman and Sara Ahmed have challenged the heteronormative ideology of this pervasive narrative in culture and politics. In his polemic book *No Future: Queer Theory and the Death Drive* (2004), Edelman challenges the politics of "reproductive futurism" and calls for a queer ethics that embraces the future-negating stance as which queer identity has been positioned within the heteronormative, future-positive order: "That Child remains the perpetual horizon of every acknowledged politics, the fantasmatic beneficiary of every political intervention."[7] Cultural and political order, Edelman argues, thus always anticipates "the Child as the image of the future it intends".[8] Choosing not to have children or failing to reproduce or to live a life in which sexuality is not ordered according to a heteronormative reproductive regime thus becomes synonymous with the negation of the future. Thus, "*queerness* names the side of those *not* 'fighting for the children', the side outside the consensus by which all politics confirms the absolute value of reproductive futurism."[9]

In *The Promise of Happiness* (2010), Sara Ahmed builds on Edelman's thesis and interprets Alfonso Cuarón's film adaptation of P. D. James' novel *Children of Men* (2006) as a film through which reproduction as the ideal of the promise of happy futures can be interrogated. The film envisions a dystopic future in which humanity is struggling with the disastrous effects of climate catastrophe, refugee crises and human infertility. No new human has been born for two decades, and most people have succumbed to fatalism, numbness and despair. News of the fatal stabbing of the youngest person on Earth—tellingly referred to as "Baby Diago" despite Diago having been 18 years old at the time of his death—is met with collective shock and grief: "no future means no children".[10] For Ahmed, the film offers ways to think about the future and hope in political struggle. Drawing on Edelman, she points out that Edelman's "inhabiting the negative" offers possibilities which, seemingly paradoxically, can be hopeful and optimistic. Queer pessimism, Ahmed points out, "matters as a pessimism *about* a certain kind of optimism, as a refusal to be optimistic about 'the right things' in the right kind of way".[11] Much like the political pessimism of the intellect promoted by Adorno and Horkheimer, then, queer pessimism as outlined by Ahmed is not a default mode but a mode of critique which helps to challenge hegemonic forms of acceptable affect and attitude. Consequently, Ahmed objects to pessimistic attitudes as "a matter of principle", which in turn might "risk being optimistic about pessimism itself".[12] Such an attitude would be a mere reflex which would lose its critical edge and become an end in itself, a compulsion rather than a subversive mode.

What particularly interests me here in Ahmed's argument for a queer pessimism is what she calls "alien affect".[13] In the context of a politics which rests on refusing to be content with what is and on putting faith in the possibilities for a better world, queer pessimism as a negation of hegemonic forms of affirmation and as an "alien affect" can become a way to rethink the present. Queer pessimism as alien affect is the expression of a refusal to feel the "right" kind of emotions about the "right" kind of things—it is, as Ahmed says, a "being for being against".[14] Coming back to Edelman, queer pessimism as alien affect can become a queer opposition to a narrative of hope which "would only reproduce the constraining mandate of futurism".[15] Queer pessimism's refusal to affirm this narrative of hope and futurity opens up new ways of thinking the future by challenging the "structuring optimism of politics".[16] It can question and refuse the politics of the "temporalization of desire", its "translation into a narrative"[17] that demands drives and desires to be in the service of socially meaningful teleological structures which culminate in the "pervasive invocation of the Child as the emblem of futurity's unquestioned value".[18] The queer-pessimistic opposition to this notion of the Child as universal futurity, and therefore the demand of every desire to be aimed at the realisation of this normative vision of futurity, is thus an "appropriately perverse refusal" in that it "will register as unthinkable, irresponsible, inhumane".[19]

Such a mode of opposition is "perverse" because its articulation of the unthinkable poses a scandal in a world dominated by the "compulsory narrative of reproductive futurism".[20] In a world which demands the sameness of sexual and heteronormative desire—a desire which always must serve a purpose for the future—such a "perverse" opposition registers as deviant. Consequently, Edelman provocatively champions the death drive as a queer mode of affirming the being against and thus appropriates the (mis)use of Freudian terminology in homophobic discourse in a gesture of subversive affirmation. Its pessimism is only truly pessimistic for those who buy into the dominant narrative of futurity. Its epistemological and ethical value, then, lies precisely in its potential for becoming a mode of critique which refuses to accept dominant narratives of the human future. Here, queer-pessimist futurity is close to Schopenhauer's thinking about time and futurity. Both Schopenhauer and the queer pessimist challenge the way linear notions of time have become the dominant a priori through which humans know themselves. Ahmed uses Schopenhauer's thinking about human desire as an optimism about fulfilled promises of happiness in the future that inevitably leads to frustration once (and if at all) the desires are satisfied. The attachment to the future in the affective structure of desire shapes human experience of time, and thus "we could say that time is what makes the future perverse".[21] This "perverse" nature of temporality is also at play in the "fetishistic fixation of heteronormativity" on visions of the future as exclusively defined and shaped by the figure of the Child.[22] Queer pessimism, then, challenges the temporality of this "compulsory narrative of reproductive futurism".[23] It thus becomes a way of prefiguring the future differently, and beyond the figure of the Child.

Queer pessimism's critique of heteronormative reproductive futurism shares similarities with antinatalist philosophies. Antinatalism as a position towards the ethical aspects of procreation is expressed to varying degrees in pessimist thought. Thomas Ligotti's *The Conspiracy Against the Human Race* suggests an antinatalist position as a reaction to the cosmic insignificance of human existence and draws on the works of Norwegian philosopher and ecologist Peter Wessel Zapffe. While Ligotti's engagement with Zapffe's thought might be more of a fringe phenomenon, antinatalism has in recent years gained some prominence in wider discussions about anthropogenic climate change. An example is the emerging BirthStrike Movement which temporarily gained some media attention.[24] The movement argues for an antinatalist lifestyle to prevent future persons from having to live in the dystopian conditions caused by global warming and ecological disaster. The underlying argument of this type of antinatalism is, then, primarily an altruistic one. What it shares with queer pessimism about reproductive futurism is its denial of heteronormative models of kinship and futurity. It is also representative of recent tendencies to rethink human impact on the environment on a planetary, species-wide scale and thus to de-centre the human to move beyond anthropocentric forms of futurity and prefiguration, as exemplified in the ecological philosophies of Timothy Morton or Patricia MacCormack.[25]

The most prominent proponent as far as philosophical positions go, however, is David Benatar's argument about antinatalism, initially laid out in *Better Never to Have Been: The Harm of Coming into Existence* (2006). Benatar makes the claim for antinatalism mainly based on his core argument about the asymmetry of pleasure and pain in all persons' lives, even the best and most fortunate ones.[26] Even the best lives, Benatar argues, have a bad quality of life, with pain, discomfort and suffering resulting from sentience outweighing life's pleasures. The ethical conclusion thus is that it is always morally wrong to reproduce and thus produce sentient life. Benatar emphasises that his argument for antinatalism does not mean to cull "worthy" lives, nor to prescribe a duty to not reproduce. His "normative premise" rather means "that one should oneself desist from bringing such beings into existence".[27] In addition to the argument that every human life brought into this world will result in the suffering of that being, Benatar adds other variables supporting his argument, including the misanthropic thesis that more human beings on earth means more exploitation and suffering of other species. Benatar arrives at his devastating conclusion about the species: "Humanity is a moral disaster. There would have been much less damage had we never evolved. The fewer humans there are in the future the less damage there will still be."[28]

What the queer pessimism of Edelman and Ahmed shares with Benatar's antinatalism is its ethical argument.[29] Taking his cue from P. D. James' novel *Children of Men*, Edelman criticises the logic of the novel, namely that there must be a "miracle birth" in the end which provides hope and redemption.[30] He proposes an alternative: "If, however, there is no baby and, in consequence, no future, then the blame must fall on the fatal lure of sterile, narcissistic enjoyments understood as inherently destructive of meaning and therefore as responsible for the undoing of social organization, collective reality, and, inevitably, life itself."[31] A "queer oppositional politics" must therefore challenge this seemingly inevitable scenario of human reproduction as the sole horizon of futurity. Ultimately then, this means to challenge the very temporality of such narratives and political visions, and hence, their teleology. The task is to challenge the "logic of a narrative wherein history unfolds as the future envisioned for a Child who must never grow up".[32] In the following sections, I will use Edelman's rigorous critique of the ideological figure of the Child as sole horizon of prefigurative action for a reading of narrative experiments with time that point to an antinatalist ethics.

"I Knew My Destination": Ted Chiang's "Story of Your Life" and Denis Villeneuve's *Arrival*

Ted Chiang's novella "Story of Your Life" (1998/2002) and Denis Villeneuve's film adaptation *Arrival* (2016) are concerned with the philosophical "paradox of future individuals",[33] or "non-identity problem",[34] which is also the basis for some of the arguments that inform David Benatar's antinatalism and its underlying thesis that coming into existence is a harm, most notably the "asymmetry argument".[35] Chiang's story and Villeneuve's film can address this paradox in the mode of science fiction. Investigating the arrival of an alien spacecraft on Earth, the linguist Dr. Louise Banks, the narrator, learns the aliens' language. Their language is intricately connected to their sense of time in that both do not function according to the human linear experience of time and language. Rather than experiencing events sequentially, the aliens experience things all at once due to their "simultaneous mode of awareness",[36] thus not adhering to human conceptions of cause and effect. The novella starts with a crucial moment in terms of the ethics of procreation: "Your father is about to ask me the question. This is the most important moment in our lives, and I want to pay attention, note every detail. [...]. And then your dad says, 'Do you want to make a baby?'"[37] Several aspects of this opening are peculiar from a narratological perspective: The second-person address is clearly directed at the homodiegetic narrator's child whose life is the titular story. What is odd about this is that the narrator seems to be able to address her child and to recount the story of her conception in the future tense. In these first paragraphs, the daughter's story already seems to be mapped out for her mother. What is more, the future tense refers to both what will happen as well as to would-be scenarios: "I'd love to tell you the story of this evening, the night you're conceived, but the right time to do that would be when you're ready to have children of your own, and we'll never get that chance."[38] This ominous sentence is a foreshadowing of what is about to happen to the narrator's daughter—as she says herself a few sentences later, "I know how this story ends."[39] The end of the story is this: the narrator knows that her daughter will die in an accident at the age of 25.[40] The story is thus revealed to be an imagined conversation between the narrator and her daughter, which is simultaneously a story of anticipation in the future tense and a retrospective account of a life lived. This narratorial paradox is epitomised in the sentence, "I'll remember a conversation we'll have when you're in your junior year in high school."[41]

The narrator remembers the future and retraces her decision to have a child despite her knowledge of the outcome.

The opening of Chiang's story even vaguely mirrors Gregory Kavka's humorous introduction to his essay on the paradox of future individuals in which he recounts the "rumor" about his own conception, compelling him to ponder the different scenarios in which the particular circumstances of his conception might not have been met and would have consequently resulted in the conception of a different individual. This "precariousness of my origin", as Kavka argues, complicates "attempts to understand our moral relationship to future generations".[42] From the vantage point of the paradox of future individuals, questions about the ethics of procreation can be explored. The most central of these questions is whether prospective parents will have a moral obligation to not have a child if they know that the child will experience more harm than good in their life. While for Benatar, coming into existence is always a harm since, as he argues, even the best lives will be full of suffering, which is dramatically underestimated, David Wasserman argues in his riposte that moral decisions about procreation should take into consideration the question whether the future child will be created as a means to an end or as an end in itself, with the value of life and the good of the future person the main priority and that beyond this, "progenitors are not morally accountable to the children they bring into existence for its unavoidable bads or goods, whatever their balance".[43] His counterargument is thus that Benatar's antinatalism primarily rests on a normative claim that does not necessarily hold true for individual and subjective evaluations of one's quality of life.[44] Wasserman instead presents two different ethical approaches to the decision of procreation, one holding "that prospective parents have a role-based duty to select the future child expected to enjoy the most well-being, or experience the least suffering"; the second denying the moral requirement of selection and holding that "as long as their lives are expected to be worth living", it is acceptable to have a child.[45] Again, the future tense ("expected to...") is central here. Debates about procreation and antinatalism (or anti-antinatalism) are based on scenarios that require the speculation and estimation of possible future scenarios, and sometimes even require an improbable scenario, such as the question whether you can ask a nonexistent future person for consent.

Denis Villeneuve's film adaptation raises the ethical stakes by having Hannah, Louise's daughter, die from an incurable illness in her early teens. Thus, in the film, her life is even shorter than in Chiang's original story, and presumably ended in greater suffering. From the perspective of an ethics of procreation, then, Louise's decision to have a child with her colleague and future husband Gary Donnelly (called Ian Donnelly in the film)[46] in the full knowledge of the future outcome is potentially even more debatable. In both the novella and the film, it is suggested that Louise's husband breaks up with her after he learns that Louise knew their daughter's fate. Thus, the two protagonists represent two ethical positions on the matter of procreation and prefiguration. While Chiang's story offers an experiment with the conventions of literary narratology to match his ethical thought experiment, Villeneuve's film resorts to forms of narrative deception through editing. Early in the film, the audience gets to see short scenes from Hannah's youth in montages that suggest they are flashbacks from Louise's past and that she had a daughter who died before the film's narrative proper starts. By playing with the audience's conventional decoding of sequential editing and montage of reaction shots, the audience is led to perceive Louise's reaction to these "flashbacks" as those of a grieving mother.

As it turns out, however, these flashbacks are indeed not flashbacks from the past, but flashforwards from the future.[47] Thus, retrospectively or upon second viewing, Louise's reactions to the "flashbacks"/flashforwards must be interpreted differently. As Anne Carruthers argues, "[a]lthough there is no way to second guess how the film makes each spectator feel, the way that the film engages the viewer through its narrative structure places ethical thinking about reproduction at the heart of the viewer's experience".[48] Crucially, the film's editing strategy produces a narrative unreliability and temporal instability which suggests "a grief that will only occur in the future".[49] Upon retrospective re-evaluation of what the audience was led to believe was a mother grieving her child's death in the past, is rather Louise's unconscious anticipation or prefiguration of future grief. This complicates how the audience (and the prospective father of her future child) morally evaluate Louise's decision to have a child despite her learning the tragic outcome. There is, then, a deliberate incongruence between what is actually happening in the film's plot, what the characters can know at a given point in time, and how the audience experiences and imagines the characters' life world as conveyed through the film's formal means. Louise's future daughter, Hannah, for instance, is as a child "conceptualized through the aesthetic of the film"[50] before she actually comes into existence in the story world. Likewise, in the source story, the daughter is anticipated as a future addressee of the narrator's account. Novella and film, through their narrative and visual means of representation, thus convey the image of a mother grieving for her future child. If, as Thomas Ligotti writes, it is strange that "[d]octors do not weep in the delivery room" over new-born children who are "falling into the future like so many bodies into open graves",[51] then Chiang's novella and Villeneuve's film imagine a scenario in which the parent can indeed already see her child's future grave.

Both "Story of Your Life" and its adaptation *Arrival* provoke the question, "should Louise knowingly give birth to someone who will die?"[52] Neither Chiang's novella nor Villeneuve's film suggests a definitive answer to this question, but they resonate with debates over the ethics of procreation from pessimist and optimist angles. If one regards "Story of Your Life" and *Arrival* in the context of Benatar and Wasserman's ethical arguments for and against antinatalism, combined with Edelman's and Ahmed's queer-pessimist intervention in the linear and progressivist narrative of reproductive futurism, then the novella and film can be regarded as complex interrogations of the ethics of reproduction. Novella and film are thought experiments that upend the temporal principles underlying reproductive futurism, but are at the same time ambivalent about the ethical conclusions to be drawn from the prefigurative conundrum the protagonist has to face. Through the narrative experiment with time and chronological order, the protagonist and her future daughter appear as embodiments of the "not-yet": the "not-yet" pregnant body, the "not-yet" born child, the "not-yet" death of the child.[53] In addition to this, then, the novella and film render their protagonist as someone who consents to and grieves the future she knows. For the readers and viewers of the story as well as for the protagonist, however, the future child as the symbol of potential and loss is already manifestly figured in the present of the narrative and the filmic image.

TIME DESTROYS ALL THINGS: GASPAR NOÉ'S *IRRÉVERSIBLE*

As several critics have pointed out, it is challenging to approach a film as immediately visceral as *Irréversible* from an adequate theoretical angle. Much has been written about the themes of the film, its sophisticated formal and stylistic construction which is in stark contrast to the affective effect it has on its viewers.[54] There is also a considerable amount of philosophical interpretations of the film, focusing on its nihilistic and existentialist themes.[55] Likewise, writers have commented on—and often angrily objected to—the presumed gender and sexual politics and its representation of identities in the film, not least its problematic depiction of gay men.[56] In the following, I want to particularly engage with the film's theme of pregnancy and its reverse narrative structure, and the implication its apodictic motto—"Time Destroys All Things"—has for these aspects of the film.[57] I will argue that the film's treatment of temporality and futurity can be read in dialogue with some of the theses on queer pessimism and queer futurity outlined earlier in this chapter. I want to further propose to read *Irréversible* as a film that is not only pessimistic about its themes but also about its own representational form. Following Eugenie Brinkema, grief is "painful *for form*", [58] and it is this idea that is realised in Noé's film. Grief as an affect aligns with pessimism in that both disrupt notions of representability: the representability of time, the representability of the not-yet, but also the representability of grief itself. This ties in with questions of aesthetic and ideological-political representation more generally. Without wanting to be apologetic about the representation of, say, queer people in Noé's film, it can be said that Noé's choices in that respect directly tie in with the film's pessimism about representability. And it is these challenges, I argue, that are addressed in Noé's confrontational film. From this vantage point, *Irréversible* can be recognised as an example of what Dienstag has called "cinema pessimism"—"a set of investigations into the representative questions that film and politics share". [59] *Irréversible* grapples with these questions about representation and representability through its form—a form that is disruptive for the viewer and at the same time itself disrupted by grief and pessimism.

While Chiang's "Story of Your Life" and Villeneuve's *Arrival* in their ambivalence also lend themselves to optimistic interpretations, it is hard to find any kind of optimism in *Irréversible*. Whereas Louise, the narrator in Chiang's story, confidently makes the decision to positively answer the question of her partner "do you want to make a baby?" in, as the reader later learns, the full awareness of her future daughter's fate, the characters in *Irréversible* do not have such foresight that could influence their decisions. Nevertheless, *Irréversible* is also concerned with the knowability of the future. The film's backward narration reverts and subverts the logic of cause and effect. Diegetically, the audience is confronted with actions that are the consequence of and reaction to events that they have not yet witnessed, the story's structure is reverted from a sequence of cause and effect into an "effect-cause system".[60] There are, however, constant cues that throughout the film refer back to events which the audience has seen and which it can subsequently make sense of. One of the foundations for this complex temporal structure is explicitly referred to by Alex, the female protagonist: on their way to the party at which she and her boyfriend Marcus will be having a falling out that will make her leave on her own and fall victim to the rapist Le Tenia ("The Tapeworm"), she mentions to Marcus and Pierre that she is currently reading *An Experiment in Time* (1927), a book of speculative philosophy and a theory of time written by the British aeronautical engineer J. W. Dunne. Dunne explores the idea of precognitive dreaming about future events, or as cases of "inverse déjà vu".[61]

Towards the end of the film (which really is the beginning of the story), Alex and Marcus are waking up from an afternoon nap. Marcus complains about his arm being numb from having twisted it during sleep (this is the same arm that one of the patrons of The Rectum will break at the "beginning" of the film), while Alex mentions a dream in which she walks through a dark tunnel (a foreshadowing of the underpass in which she will be assaulted by Le Tenia). *Irréversible* is thus "a line of dominoes falling in reverse",[62] but its protagonists are tragically unaware of the things that await them in their near future. For the audience, however, every element in the diegetic past becomes a "complex of reverse-pointing cues" so that the diegesis seems like a "flotsam and jetsam of narrative debris".[63] The film thus forces the audience to experience its titular irreversibility as a downward spiral of chaos and destruction. The film's motto—"time destroys all things"—is thus enacted by the film's structure. However, the motto also points to a more nuanced interpretation. It is a loose translation of a line from Ovid's *Metamorphoses*—"tempus edax rerum",[64] which can be translated more accurately as "time devours all things". The verse features a description of the cycle of life from conception and birth to old age and death. What is crucial here, however, is that Ovid relates this cycle to a wider cosmology which also entails the interrelationship of all living and dying matter and equally implies rebirth, even if it is in a different shape and form.

It would be a stretch to call Noé's bleak vision utopian, but even if his radical deconstruction of narrative conventions subjects its human protagonists to relentless destruction, with the drastic smashing of faces as a recurring motif that suggests the complete obliteration of individual human identities, its upending of conventional notions of linear temporality offers room for hopeful interpretations from a cosmic perspective. This becomes clearer in the re-edited "straight cut" of the film which was released in 2019. Put into a more conventional causal narrative, the straight cut ends with a slightly altered motto, now reading "Le temps révèle tout" (Time reveals all things). What new nuance does this add to the film's unrelenting philosophy? It links *Irréversible* even closer to pessimist conceptions of temporality, most notably Schopenhauer's metaphysical discussion of time and the will-to-live. For Schopenhauer, time is the core category which constitutes human's consciousness and being. Time consciousness is inextricable from what he perceives as the misery of human existence: the regretful awareness of the past and the things that could have been and the equally negative awareness of the future and the finite nature of one's existence. This awareness leads to the predicament that the only register of real experience, the present moment, is barely noticed: "*Time* and the *fleeting nature* of all things-therein, and by means thereof, are merely the form wherein is revealed to the will-to-live, which as the thing-in-itself is imperishable, the *vanity* of that striving. *Time* is that by virtue whereof at every moment all things in our hands come to nought and thereby lose all true value."[65] For Schopenhauer, the fleeting nature of life makes, as Joshua Foa Dienstag observes, the real metaphysical "knowledge of the thing-in-itself" virtually impossible.[66] The only way to come close to such true knowledge is to imagine "a world without the a prioris, which means, above all, a world without linear time".[67]

Noé's deconstruction of linear narrative time and also his hyperreal sense of space, with the camera frequently offering unnatural perspectives and omnisciently swirling and sometimes worming its way through space and time, can thus be said to offer an attempt to undo these a prioris that keep humans from true knowledge. It can also be seen as the depiction of Schopenhauer's characterisation of a person's course of life: "having been duped by hope, they dance into the arms of death".[68] The journey of the characters in *Irréversible* reflects this fatal dance. The fleeting nature of human happiness is evident during the house party scene. At the party, Alex briefly sits down with a visibly pregnant friend; when watching the original cut of the film, the audience at this point is not yet aware of Alex' own pregnancy, but she hints at this when she promises her pregnant friend to catch up with her in the coming days, declaring that she is intent on enjoying herself that night since it is "a special day" and that she is happy. As the audience later realises, she has just learned of her own pregnancy shortly before leaving for the party. Lit in warm colours and showing people enjoying themselves in either chatting, trance-like collective dancing, or having sex, the party scene seems like a utopian counterimage to the hellscape of the Rectum earlier in the film. Alex's happiness, however, is fleeting, as her boyfriend Marcus, unaware of her pregnancy, spoils her night with his rude and selfish behaviour which makes her leave the party on her own. This fatal turn not only illustrates the fleeting nature of happiness—rendered in Schopenhauerian terms as merely a "temporary absence of suffering"[69]—but is also the moment that leads to Alex heading towards her fate.

As in "Story of Your Life" and *Arrival*, the embodiment of the (not-yet) pregnant woman and the figuration of the Child is central to the corporeal strategy of *Irréversible*. The figure of the child Alex is bearing is allegorically present in the form of a poster of Stanley Kubrick's film *2001: A Space Odyssey* (1968) showing the Star-Child visible in Alex and Marcus' apartment and appearing to watch over the protagonists right before Alex realises she is pregnant. As one of cinema history's central symbols of (re) birth, transcendence and cosmic existence,[70] Kubrick's Star-Child suggests the possibility of a different futurity and temporality in *Irréversible*.

Noé's film contrasts this transcendental iconography of the Child as the telos of heterosexual reproductive futurism with what is arguably one of its most controversial aspects: its depiction of Alex's rapist as a gay man and his regular haunt, the BDSM club Rectum. Here, the film runs the risk of stigmatising and exploiting stereotypical images of "deviant" male homosexuality, not least because the film's straight male protagonists display homophobia and outright hostility towards any queer characters they encounter. However, if seen in the context of a disruption of dominant heteronormative notions of family, procreation and temporal linearity, the film's depiction of the gay BDSM subculture becomes a hyperbolic nightmarish manifestation of its protagonists' phobias and resentments. It becomes the antithesis to what the heterosexual men in the film hold dear: "If the well-being of the Child is guaranteed by heterosexual family and reproduction, queerness figures as its fundamental threat."[71] Thus, if read with Edelman and other scholars of queer negativity, Noé's disruption of the temporal order of reproductive futurism consciously plays with such perceived threats to heteronormativity. The aesthetic experience (not the production, which is quite carefully structured and composed) of the film as a whole is visceral, pre-rational and instinctual—it is an affective experience first and foremost, and the viewer experiences the temporal unsettling as a profoundly disorienting event: *Irréversible* is an audiovisual assault. The same goes for the straight characters in the film who enter a world beyond their cultural norms which presents itself to the viewer not as a representation of "reality" with any markers of cinematic realism but as a hyperreal nightmarish fantasy. Their instinct is to fight and extinguish

this culture, as can be seen in the misguided act of vengeance and vigilan-
tism. What the two straight men want to accomplish with this act of violence is not just to avenge a crime but to punish the notion of queerness
itself, an attempt to eradicate the threat to one's norms. Thus, it does not
so much matter whether the victim is actually the rapist (he is not), but
within the value system that the two straight men want to defend, virtually
any of the men they encounter in the club is, in their sacrificial logic, a
suitable victim. At the same time, and this is the point that Noé's film
makes quite bluntly, the very values that are supposed to be defended are
exposed to be precarious and quickly evaporate when put to the test in a
violent confrontation. Simply put, by destroying another man's body
(obliterating his face), one's very own values (civilisation, culture, justice)
are being destroyed—or rather, they are exposed as having always been a
mere veneer, to begin with. Time destroys everything, including one's
ethical values or pretensions thereof. In that respect, to come back to Sara
Ahmed, Noé drastically demonstrates that time makes the future perverse.[72]

Noé thus takes seriously the notion that from the perspective of heteronormative reproductive futurity, queer people represent a "a culture of
death".[73] Drawing on Lee Edelman's *No Future* and at the same time
resisting it, Heather Love has proposed to read queer histories as structures of feeling in a backward sense. For her, queer histories, which are
often rooted in past trauma, stigma and violence, pose a challenge to projects of futurity. On the one hand, queer people want to reclaim their identities and their histories from the catastrophe of the past; on the other, that
past inevitably haunts such desires for futurity. Love thus interprets this
struggle over queer narratives as an essential experience of modernity:
"The idea of modernity—with its suggestions of progress, rationality, and
technological advance—is intimately bound up with backwardness."[74] This
dialectic of progress and regress is for Love epitomised in the queer subject
who needs to come to terms with a violent and traumatic past and needs to
reclaim their identity for the future in a "reverse discourse".[75] Love identifies allegorical figurations of this "feeling backward" in Walter Benjamin's
"Angel of History" who cannot look to the future because his gaze is fixed
backwards to the accumulating debris of history's catastrophes, "an
emblem of resistance to the forward march of progress".[76] However, the
Angel also "longs to redeem the past" and refuses to see the debris of historical catastrophe as merely the material of progress.[77] This "temporal
splitting" is not only central for the experience of historical modernity but
at the heart of all aesthetic modernism.[78] Rather than suspending the

"question of the future" as Edelman does in *No Future*, Love, while acknowledging the importance of Edelman's radical project, is "interested in trying to imagine a future apart from the reproductive imperative, optimism, and the promise of redemption. A backward future, perhaps".[79]

Coming back to the problem of gay representation in Noé's *Irréversible*, one can detect many of the arguments that Love addresses in *Feeling Backward*. Seen in this context, *Irréversible*'s representation of male homosexuality is still ambivalent at best and disturbing and downright homophobic at worst. But taking into consideration that the film's narrative struggles with very similar issues of precarious temporality as Edelman and Love, and if its reverse narration and its emphasis on the irreversibility of that which is destroyed in and by time is seen as a similar attempt to come to terms with a "feeling backward", with an attempt to not let go of the traumatic catastrophe by placing its cataclysmic conclusion at the very beginning of the film, another possible interpretation of its representations emerges. If the Rectum and its sexual excess are considered as the antithesis to heterosexual reproductive sexuality as well as the manifestation of a particular kind of middle-class heterosexual homophobic paranoia (most clearly represented by the overly virile Marcus and his constant homophobic, transphobic and racist slurs), then the film's representation of gay men can be read as a darkly comedic manifestation of Marcus' homophobia. The Rectum sequence seems to spell out Leo Bersani's provocative question in the 1980s at the height of the HIV/AIDS crisis: "Is the rectum a grave?" (1987). Bersani argued that if for a heteronormative culture "the rectum is the grave in which the masculine ideal (an ideal shared—differently—by men *and* women) of proud subjectivity is buried, then it should be celebrated for its very potential for death".[80] Bersani goes on to argue that, in a tragic way, the HIV/AIDS crisis has

> literalized that potential as the certainty of biological death, and has therefore reinforced the heterosexual association of anal sex with a self-annihilation originally and primarily identified with the fantasmatic mystery of an insatiable, unstoppable female sexuality. It may, finally, be in the gay man's rectum that he demolishes his own perhaps otherwise uncontrollable identification with a murderous judgment against him.[81]

Bersani here addresses the ambivalent meanings of anal sex within a heteronormative matrix of acceptable and unacceptable sexual practices, with anal sex at the same time being the ultimate taboo for the homophobic straight man, and by the same token, a fantasmatic image of desire. In *Irréversible*, this also figures in Marcus' absurd battle cry "we're going to the Rectum!" when he embarks on his mission for vengeance.[82] Marcus' battle cry sounds both aggressive and threatening (he is intent on killing his girlfriend's rapist) and strangely anticipatory. Marcus ends up with the Rectum's patron mistaken for Le Tenia, raping him anally and breaking his arm, and with Pierre coming to the rescue, smashing the assailant's skull to a pulp, and thus literally turning the Rectum into a grave. Robin Wood, who offered a dialectic reading of the film's difficult representation of gay masculinity, describes the "the Rectum's 'Hell'" as "a vivid representation of masculinity gone insane, the ultimate expression of masculinism's worst extremes", with "gay men as violent and insatiable predators".[83] Wood is concerned that the message of the film could be read as: "sex is for procreation! Those who disagree will go to Hell, the ultimate Hell being preserved for men who carry their disagreement to its logical conclusion."[84] However, the film's seemingly straightforward trajectory from Heaven (heterosexual procreation, the Child as emblem of the future) to Hell (nonreproductive, all-male destructive sexuality) is complicated by the fact that "[w]e cannot understand *Irreversible*, or appreciate its qualities and complexities, unless we are willing patiently to reconstruct its twelve sequences in chronological order. Even the relationship between the film and its title demands thought: 'Time', which 'destroys everything' is irreversible, yet the structure (defiantly? ironically?) *reverses* Time."[85]

This aporetic dynamic echoes Heather Love's interpretation of Benjamin's "Angel of History" as an allegory of feeling backward. *Irréversible*'s structure echoes Benjamin's Angel who sees the storm of progress coming but cannot avert his gaze from the debris of history's catastrophes behind him. Both Benjamin's Angel and *Irréversible* perform a "temporal splitting" which is not only central for the experience of historical modernity but at the heart of all aesthetic modernism.[86] When the film concludes with the final swirling and sped-up idyllic images of Alex lying on the lawn, knowing that she is pregnant, with children playing around her, this image, like Benjamin's Angel of History, becomes an allegory of the directionality of time. Like the storm of progress coming towards the Angel of History, the speeding-up of the image signals the pregnant woman as being torn between the catastrophe that awaits (and that the audience has already seen in its backwards-movement) and the horizon of future possibilities she and her child could have awaited her instead.[87]

Ethics, Grief and Representational Form

Antinatalism concerns the ethics of reproduction on a personal and individual level. It starts from a pessimist assessment of the world, and of the quality of life in this world. According to this pessimist assessment, suffering outweighs pleasure and the benefits of being alive. Human beings suffer themselves, and it is therefore a harm to bring them into existence. Likewise, these future humans might inflict suffering on fellow human beings and other species, and thus negatively impact ecosystems on a planetary scale. The practical ethical conclusion is to decide against procreation, at least on a personal level. Benatar and other antinatalists' arguments echo Schopenhauer's thoughts on suffering. Schopenhauer goes further in his conclusions for behaviour in that he rejects the idea of happiness as an achievable goal in life. For Schopenhauer, the personal consequence should be to resign in the face of the unattainability of sustainable, lasting happiness. The "promise of happiness" will most likely result in frustration and, therefore, unhappiness. To not expect happiness might alleviate this frustration. Schopenhauer's call for a stoical attitude that does not expect happiness is the closest his philosophy comes to eudaemonism, that is, to a concept of what leading a good life could look like. As Joshua Foa Dienstag has argued, Schopenhauer's stoicism is ethical only on a secondary level. It is a side-effect of the stoic attitude which might lead to certain kinds of ethical behaviour, but it does not amount to an ethical framework that could apply to humanity as a whole.[88]

So what ethical conclusions can be drawn from the fictional narratives by Ted Chiang, Denis Villeneuve and Gaspar Noé? Is there an ethics of procreation to be found in these narratives featuring pregnant female protagonists who are challenged with the obstacles of time? Ted Chiang's science fiction scenario foregoes the paradox of future persons that antinatalist philosophy has to reconcile since the protagonist of "Story of Your Life" and Villeneuve's adaptation *Arrival* literally knows the future life of her yet unborn daughter and how it will end prematurely. Does Chiang and Villeneuve's protagonist commit an ethically irresponsible act by choosing to reproduce? The answer is complicated by the question of agency in the face of the hypothetical scenario of being able to know the future. Louise's decision to have a child despite her knowledge of the future might be considered as a form of neglectful optimism. But maybe, to return to Schopenhauer, she acts even more in line with the ethical implications of pessimist thought. She has stoically accepted the course of time even in the full knowledge of future pain. It is also significant that in the short story, it is the future father who asks his partner, "do you want to make a baby?", which she affirms. Both partners enact, as it were, a script: As Louise tells her future daughter at the end of Chiang's novella: "From the beginning I knew my destination, and I chose my route accordingly. But am I working toward an extreme of joy, or of pain?"[89] This question might be easy to answer from the perspectives of Benatar's normative analysis of life and Schopenhauer's absolutist metaphysical pessimism, but it remains an open one for Louise, who might know her future but cannot yet know the affects of a life not yet lived.

The story's mode of science fiction touches on another ethical question: does the knowledge of the future allow or even compel us to interfere with the course of future events? From a pessimist perspective, the question is whether it would even matter. If it would mean to disrupt the equilibrium of time, it would merely have a temporary effect. But the overall challenge at the heart of all pessimist thinking which is, as Dienstag has argued, to come to terms with the harrowing repercussions of human time consciousness[90] would not be alleviated. Certain events could be altered or prevented which might temporarily alleviate potential suffering and avert catastrophe, but it would not change the overall crushing effect of time.

The pessimist ethics of *Irréversible* are best identified when looking at the issue of happiness in the film. Alex says that she is "happy" when she talks to her pregnant friend at the party. This is before we see her looking at her pregnancy test result and sitting under Kubrick's Star-Child, and before we see her lying in the park, reading *An Experiment with Time*. Those first/last moments of the film are its true utopian moments. But the bliss is already fleeting in the very moment she says the words "I'm happy". Seeing that Marcus acts increasingly recklessly, dancing with other women and taking drugs, ruining the mood and compelling Alex to angrily leave the party on her own. Her "promise of happiness" is not fulfilled. This is in line with Schopenhauer's deconstruction of the idea of happiness and the human desire to pursue it. Marcus' constant narcissistic striving for jouissance and self-gratification conflict with Alex's sense of happiness (even though, ironically, she had earlier told her ex-boyfriend Pierre the secret for true sexual gratification: rather than constantly thinking about his partner's pleasure, which would keep both him and his partner from experiencing pleasure, he should have sex egoistically). As

Dienstag points out, Schopenhauer "advises us to be free from the demands of one's desire".[91] Thus, if there is a deeper pessimist ethics in the film, it would be the same kind of secondary ethics which Dienstag describes as the indirect result of Schopenhauer's attitude of letting be.

Finally, I want to return to the initial question whether one can mourn the future. Following Eugenie Brinkema, I argue that Chiang, Villeneuve and Noé's narratives move beyond mourning (which would still offer the dialectics of productively working through loss) to a stage of grieving for the future (as an affect that is unproductive, traumatic and undialectical). Both "Story of Your Life" and *Irréversible* grapple with the fact that time will destroy all things. Both use the pregnant woman as an embodiment of a precarious futurity. The unborn Child, much like it has been criticised by queer pessimists, serves as the figuration of a telos, a notion of futurity. Crucially, however, the Child as a figure is absent in both narratives and only insinuated as a future addressee (in Chiang's story), as a visual glimpse of the future (in Villeneuve's film) or as an idea metonymically alluded to by Kubrick's Star-Child (in Noé's film). Through this representational deferral, the unborn or not-yet-born child becomes the absent centre of a grief for the future. In that, the narratives resonate with antinatalism and queer pessimism as challenges to thinking time and the future.

As Eugenie Brinkema has argued, grief is something more traumatic than mourning in that it constitutes a pain that cannot be productively worked through and thus is a traumatic disruption of forms and texts of narrative and visual representation: "the dimension of grief moves as something that is painful *for form*".[92] In that, grief cannot be resolved in a productive dialectics—it is fundamentally undialectical.[93] Chiang, Villeneuve and Noé's narratives of reproduction revolve around such traumatic wounds to representational form in their disruptions of narrated time and the affected bodies of their protagonists. Thus, they find forms to make the future "grievable". Grief, Brinkema argues, "poses a unique set of problems for any system of representation predicated on presencing: tarrying with grief requires representation to negotiate an affect that results from a loss and thus requires representation to invent a visual vocabulary for the in-visible absent".[94] "Story of Your Life", *Arrival* and *Irréversible* inventively confront the representational challenge of future loss and the loss of the future. In that, they not only convey the trauma of grief to representational form. Rather, they take this grief as the starting point for a pessimism of representational form.

Notes

1. Eva Horn, *The Future as Catastrophe: Imagining Disaster in the Modern Age* (New York: Columbia University Press, 2018).
2. *First Reformed*, directed by Paul Schrader (A24, 2017).
3. Adeline Johns-Putra, *Climate Change and the Contemporary Novel* (Cambridge: Cambridge University Press, 2019), p. 57.
4. Johns-Putra, 2019, p. 59.
5. Johns-Putra, 2019, p. 68.
6. See Judith Butler, *Precarious Life: The Powers of Mourning and Violence* (London: Verso, 2006).
7. Lee Edelman, *No Future: Queer Theory and the Death Drive* (Durham: Duke University Press, 2004), p. 3.
8. Edelman, 2004, p. 3.
9. Edelman, 2004, p. 3, emphasis in original.
10. Sara Ahmed, *The Promise of Happiness* (Durham: Duke University Press, 2010), p. 164.
11. Ahmed, 2010, p. 162, emphasis in original.
12. Ahmed, 2010, p. 162.
13. Ahmed, 2010, p. 162.
14. Ahmed, 2010, p. 162.
15. Edelman, 2004, p. 4.
16. Edelman, 2004, p. 5.
17. Edelman, 2004, p. 9.
18. Edelman, 2004, p. 3.
19. Edelman, 2004, p. 4.
20. Edelman, 2004, p. 21.
21. Ahmed, 2010, p. 180.
22. Edelman, 2004, p. 21.
23. Edelman, 2004, p. 21.
24. Elle Hunt, "BirthStrikers: Meet the Women Who Refuse to Have Children until Climate Change Ends", *The Guardian*, 12 March 2019.
25. Cf. Timothy Morton, *Dark Ecology: For a Logic of Future Coexistence* (New York: Columbia University Press, 2016); Patricia MacCormack, *The Ahuman Manifesto: Activism for the End of the Anthropocene* (London: Bloomsbury, 2020).; see also chapter 5 for a more extensive discussion of Morton and MacCormack.
26. David Benatar, *Better Never to Have Been: The Harm of Coming Into Existence* (Oxford: Oxford University Press, 2006), pp. 30–39.
27. David Benatar and David Wasserman, *Debating Procreation: Is It Wrong to Reproduce?* (Oxford: Oxford University Press, 2015), p. 101, emphasis in original.
28. Benatar & Wasserman, 2015, p. 111.

29. See Edelman's argument about ethical value of queerness (2004, p. 5).
30. Edelman, 2004, pp. 11–12.
31. Edelman, 2004, p. 13.
32. Edelman, 2004, p. 21.
33. Gregory S. Kavka, "The Paradox of Future Individuals", *Philosophy & Public Affairs* 11, no. 2 (1982): 93–112.
34. Derek Parfit, *Reasons and Persons* (Oxford: Clarendon Press, 1984), p. 359. See David Benatar, 2006, p. 19 and in Benatar/Wasserman 2015, pp. 18–19 for a detailed discussion of this paradox.
35. Benatar, 2006, pp. 18–19.
36. Ted Chiang, "Story of Your Life", in *Stories of Your Life and Others* (London: Picador, 2020), 109–72, p. 159.
37. Chiang, 2020, p. 111.
38. Chiang, 2020, p. 111.
39. Chiang, 2020, p. 112.
40. Chiang, 2020, p. 116.
41. Chiang, 2020, p. 129.
42. Kavka, 1982, p. 93.
43. Benatar & Wasserman, 2015, p. 137.
44. Benatar & Wasserman, 2015, p. 138.
45. Benatar & Wasserman, 2015, p. 144.
46. *Arrival*, directed by Denis Villeneuve (Paramount, 2016).
47. Anne Carruthers, "Temporality, Reproduction and the Not-Yet in Denis Villeneuve's Arrival", *Film-Philosophy*, no. 22:3 (2018): 321–39, p. 333.
48. Carruthers, 2018, p. 329.
49. Carruthers, 2018, p. 330.
50. Carruthers, 2018, p. 335.
51. Thomas Ligotti, *The Conspiracy Against the Human Race: A Contrivance of Horror* (New York: Hippocampus Press, 2010), pp. 227–228.
52. Carruthers, 2018, p. 338.
53. Carruthers, 2018, p. 338.
54. For an overview, see Tim Palmer, *Irreversible* (New York: Palgrave, 2015), p. 69.
55. See Eric Migernier, "Rape as Irreversible Violence: An Existentialist Interpretation", *SISS II: The Image of Violence in Literature, Media, and Society*, 2007, 108–11.
56. Palmer, 2015, pp. 110–111 and Robin Wood, "Against and For Irreversible", *Film International*, 5 April 2011, n. p.
57. *Irréversible,* directed by Gaspar Noé (StudioCanal, Mars Distribution, 2002).
58. Eugenie Brinkema, *The Forms of the Affects* (Durham: Duke University Press, 2014), p. 93, emphasis in original.

59. Joshua Foa Dienstag, *Cinema Pessimism: A Political Theory of Representation and Reciprocity* (Oxford: Oxford University Press, 2020), p. 12.
60. Palmer, 2015, p. 72.
61. Palmer, 2015, p. 73.
62. Palmer, 2015, p. 73.
63. Palmer, 2015, p. 72.
64. Ovid, *Metamorphoses*, Book XV, Verse 234.
65. Arthur Schopenhauer, *On the Suffering of the World*, ed. Eugene Thacker (London: Repeater, 2020), p. 91.
66. Dienstag, 2020, p. 89.
67. Dienstag, 2006, p. 89.
68. Schopenhauer, 2020, p. 95.
69. Benatar, 2006, p. 77.
70. Cf. Suparno Banerjee: "2001: A Space Odyssey: A Transcendental Trans-Locution", *Understanding Kubrick's 2001: A Space Odyssey: Representation and Interpretation*, ed. James Fenwick. (Bristol: Intellect, 2020), 33–44, p. 38.
71. Cedric Essi, "Queer Futurity", in *Critical Terms in Futures Studies*, ed. Heike Paul (Houndsmills: Palgrave, 2019), 245–51, p. 246.
72. Ahmed, 2010, p. 180.
73. Edelman, 2004, p. 39.
74. Heather Love, *Feeling Backward Loss and the Politics of Queer History* (Cambridge, MA: Harvard University Press, 2009), p. 5.
75. Love, 2007, p. 2.
76. Love, 2007, p. 147.
77. Love, 2007, p. 148.
78. Love, 2007, p. 6.
79. Love, 2007, p. 147.
80. Leo Bersani, "Is the Rectum a Grave?", *October*, no. 43 (1987): 197–222, p. 222.
81. Bersani, 1987, p. 222.
82. *Irréversible*, 2002.
83. Wood 2011, n. p.
84. Wood 2011, n. p.
85. Wood, 2011, n. p.
86. Love, 2007, p. 6.
87. Cf. Also Eric Migernier, "Rape as Irreversible Violence: An Existentialist Interpretation", *SISS II: The Image of Violence in Literature, Media, and Society*, 2007: 108–11, p. 111.
88. Dienstag, 2006, p. 111.

89. Chiang, 2020, p. 172.
90. Dienstag, 2006, pp. 9–16.
91. Dienstag, 2006, p. 111.
92. Brinkema, 2014, p. 93, emphasis in original.
93. Brinkema, 2014, p. 92.
94. Brinkema, 2014, p. 94.

CHAPTER 5

Embracing the Apocalypse: Extinction, Cosmic Pessimism and Ahuman Futures

Abstract The radical questioning of life and existence in the face of an apocalyptic horizon of extinction reflects the current conjuncture's cultural logic of the worst and its radical questioning of temporality. This observation is supported by the proliferation of such pessimist-speculative ideas in the cultural arena beyond philosophical circles. In recent years, there has been an emergence of more radical apocalyptic fictions in which the end of the world or the human species is not averted at the last minute. Fictional imaginaries of apocalypse and extinction constitute a cultural epistemology of pessimism from which to tackle the fundamental concerns of the present and future of the Anthropocene. The prospect of extinction can be a useful vantage point of such a pessimist epistemology. This chapter discusses extinctionism and apocalypse as paradigms in the cosmic pessimism of Thomas Ligotti and the ahuman theory of Patricia MacCormack and explores how these ideas resonate in Lars von Trier's film *Melancholia* (2011) and Camille Griffin's film *Silent Night* (2021). Like the philosophy of Ligotti and MacCormack, these films prefigure futures beyond the human.

Keywords Extinction • Apocalypse • Cosmic Pessimism • Ahuman theory • Patricia MacCormack • Camille Griffin • Lars von Trier • Thomas Ligotti • Eugene Thacker

AGAINST LIFE

Life should not be—this is, according to Thomas Ligotti, the most funda-mental premise of pessimism. With this statement, Ligotti points to a tra-dition of existential pessimism that is indebted as much to Arthur Schopenhauer's prominent pessimist philosophy as to the thinking of more obscure thinkers such as the antinatalist Peter Wessel Zapffe. The contention that "life is something that should not be" and that what "*should* be is the absence of life, nothing, non-being, the emptiness of the uncreated"[1] is categorical and absolute. There are no grey areas or degrees to this definition of pessimism—and, by exclusion, optimism: "Anyone who speaks up for life as something that irrefutably should be—that we should *not* be better off unborn, extinct, or forever lazing in nonexis-tence—is an optimist."[2] This view of pessimism, then, goes further than most of the pessimisms discussed in previous chapters in that it denies, first, any kind of usefulness that one might still find in the appropriations of pessimism for political ends, such as in Max Horkheimer, Theodor Adorno and Stuart Hall. Second, it consequently also precludes any kind of dialectics. Instead, the pessimism outlined by Ligotti is pure negation. By contrast, Ligotti takes into consideration what he sarcastically refers to as the "never-say-die group" of "heroic 'pessimists'".[3] Including writers such as Miguel de Unamuno, Albert Camus, William R. Brashear and Joshua Foa Dienstag, this branch of pessimists, as it were, adulterates absolutist pessimism by trying to use it as a perspective "to meet existence more than halfway" and "marches on toward a future believed to be per-sonally and politically workable".[4]

One could extend Ligotti's list of "heroic" would-be pessimists by including many of the thinkers discussed in this present book, and it can certainly be expected that Ligotti would strongly object to the usefulness of pessimism in the wider project of cultural studies, whether it is to be found in its objects of analysis or in its wider political project as outlined in my introduction and in the first chapter. So the question is whether cultural studies, especially if understood (as I have explored in Chap. 2) as a political project concerned with the study of cultural artefacts from a materialist and Marxist perspective, can be reconciled with a body of thought that is, to put it bluntly, deliberately antisystematic, unconstruc-tive if not destructive and defeatist? One could object that this would be a futile exercise since each attempt at reconciliation could eventually, from a Ligottian perspective, be derided as a perpetuation of life's lies and a delusional reaffirmation that "being alive is all right".[5] The Gramscian pessimism of the intellect of cultural studies theorists such as Stuart Hall would, from this perspective, merely amount to an attempt at "heroic pessimism". And yet, as I will argue in this chapter, this absolutist, anti-life pessimism offers important lessons for a cultural studies which wants to tend to the current conjuncture.

Ligotti is not alone in his absolutist pessimism that, apart from the forebears he refers to in his own book *The Conspiracy Against the Human Race*, can also be found in Eugene Thacker's cosmic pessimism as well as in the scientific nihilism of Ray Brassier. In these writers' works, negation and extinction are correlates within the "logics of the worst".[6] Like Ligotti, Thacker and Brassier address the horror of thinking and being by confronting not merely the finitude of the thinking individual, but indeed of the whole human species and of all terrestrial life. Such a thinking seeks to de-centre the human in a planetary (and sometimes cosmic) context and thus can be said to follow a mode of pessimist thinking epitomised by Schopenhauer's philosophy in *The World as Will and Representation*. This de-centring breaks with human–world correlations as a "world-for-us" and takes on the challenge to think a "world-without-us"[7] and even a "life *without us*".[8] In a similar way, the end of the world and the death of species figure as a horizon of thought in the work of Timothy Morton. The notion of the end of the world is central to Morton's radical rethinking of the ontological certainties about humans' relationship with ecology, the environment and "hyperobjects" that transcend spatiotemporal frames, like climate change or the biosphere. Morton's Object-Oriented Ontology thus relies on similar axioms as that of pessimists like Ligotti and Thacker. It is also close to what Patricia MacCormack calls becoming "ahuman".[9] In MacCormack's fundamentally misanthropic worldview, humans are only an exceptional species for the fact that they are the singularly most destructive and deadly force on the planet. Therefore, to acknowledge humanity's place within the wider ecology of the planet, they need to take responsibility by ceasing to reproduce and minimise their damaging impact on the species they share a planet with. For MacCormack, the end of the world, or apocalypse, is central since she contrasts the anthropocentric fear of "the great, single apocalypse that will wipe us all out" with the many individual microcosmic apocalypses for minoritarian beings, whether they be precarious human lives or nonhuman lives, that are already happening each moment.[10] Thus, she hails an apocalypse that would bring an end to anthropocentric dominion: "What would be so terrible to be wiped out of a world which many already negotiate as dystopic at best and post-apocalyptic at worst?"[11] The pessimist dictum that life should not be is reiterated here, although MacCormack makes it clear that it is human life that should not be so that nonhuman life can flourish.

The thinkers I outlined so far might not necessarily explicitly subscribe to pessimism as their philosophical frameworks,[12] but they are nevertheless united by shared premises and axioms that have their roots in the negational stance of metaphysical or cosmic pessimism, as outlined by Ligotti and Thacker. What they also share is their approach to (human) extinction, the end of the world, of being, of thought as speculative horizons that compel us to rethink not only our own ontological status as species and our entanglements with other species but indeed the very notions of being and life in the face of finitude. The proliferation of such thinking could in parts be considered as a reaction to a growing and wide-ranging awareness of ecological issues in the face of the climate and environmental crisis, a crisis which can no longer be ignored and which necessitates the rethinking of human impact on a planetary scale. Morton and MacCormack address these issues most explicitly, with MacCormack considering her ahuman thinking as part of a new form of ethical activism. These concerns might not necessarily be shared by a writer like Ligotti, but the fact that there are philosophical continuities between the ecological thought of Morton and MacCormack and pessimists like Ligotti and Thacker speaks to my notion of a pessimist conjuncture outlined in previous chapters.

The radical questioning of life and existence in the face of an apocalyptic horizon of extinctionism reflects the current conjuncture's cultural logic of the worst and its radical questioning of temporality. This observation is supported by the proliferation of such pessimist-speculative ideas in the cultural arena beyond philosophical circles. Disaster fiction might be a staple of blockbuster cinema (think Roland Emmerich or Michael Bay), but in recent years, there has been an emergence of more radical apocalyptic fiction in which the end of the world or the human species is not averted at the last minute. Fictional imaginaries of apocalypse and extinction constitute a cultural epistemology of pessimism from which to tackle the fundamental concerns of the present and future of the Anthropocene. The prospect of extinction can be a useful vantage point of such a pessimist epistemology. In this chapter, I will discuss examples of such extinctionist fiction to explore the potential of their cosmic and extinctionist pessimism for cultural studies.

This chapter will focus on Lars von Trier's film *Melancholia* (2011) and Camille Griffin's film *Silent Night* (2021) in the context of a discussion of extinctionist philosophies. These films' apocalyptic imagination does not shy away from actually having the world (or humanity) come to an end. Their cosmic pessimism ultimately provides a perspective looking towards what comes after the future,[13] after the human,[14] after life.[15] Cosmic and extinctionist pessimism points to what comes after the human world and temporality of the Anthropocene. It imagines a world which was not made for us, and in doing so, it addresses crucial issues relevant for cultural studies and prefiguration.

THINKING EXTINCTION

In both, his thus far only philosophical[16] work *The Conspiracy Against the Human Race* as well as in his horror fiction, Thomas Ligotti interrogates human conceptions of life and being against the horizon of existence as a "malignantly useless"[17] state. From his cosmic-pessimist perspective, human consciousness appears as an evolutionary misstep that only accentuates the futility of existence. Scoffing at ideas of Self and subjectivity, for Ligotti, human existence is merely the life of a puppet that imagines itself to be someone, a person, a self. His antihumanist thinking figures human existence as that of an "uncharacter",[18] which is thrown around by instinct and arbitrarily tossed around by an indifferent cosmos. His short story "The Nightmare Network" is a variation of this idea with an anticapitalist bend: The story envisions a huge corporation, called Oneiricon ("The nightmare of the past becomes the dream of the future: Oneiricon—one world, one dream"),[19] which perfects human labour exploitation into overdrive. The corporation's rhetoric is a parody of neoliberal advertising:

> Our enterprise is now thriving in a tough, global marketplace and has taken on a life all its own. If you are a committed, focused individual with a hunger to be part of something far greater than yourself... our door is now open. Your life need not be a nightmare of failure and resentment. Join us. Outstanding benefits.[20]

However, once the corporation has destroyed all its competitors on the galactic marketplace, it must resort to creating "puppet entities" to create an artificial competition: "Project Puppetcorps". Ligotti's story jumps back and forth in time to evoke an image of capitalist competition as a transhistorical principle. It is also a paradoxical principle: capitalism thrives on competition and merging, and therefore its principle of continuous growth relies on invading other organisations and individual organisms, much like the shape-shifting alien in John Carpenter's film *The Thing* (1982). The corporation relies on destroying others, yet stasis or ungrowth spell degeneration. In this vision of the world, capitalism has become an all-encompassing, universal apocalyptic principle. One last merger with its last competitor, the Nightmare Network, might stave off degeneration. The Nightmare Network is the pessimistic antithesis to the capitalist optimism of Oneiricon:

> the Nightmare Network, where individuals and collective values tend towards subversion without regard for rational pretexts. All of them being natural-born losers and self-destructive organisms of the worst sort, they run crotch-first into bargain, some even adopting multiple identities so that they can experience more than once the monstrous thrill of selling out their own futile aspirations.[21]

The Nightmare Network infiltrates other organisations to destroy them from within. It can thus be read as what Scott Sandage has called the "hidden history of pessimism" in American capitalism's "culture of optimism".[22] As Sandage and Jack Halberstam[23] have respectively argued, the capitalist ideal of individual aspiration, optimism and success always produces an untold history of failure—something which could be called the nightside of capitalist success, a history of stasis and decline. As an anti-corporation of "natural-born losers", the Nightmare Network practices the "art of failure" that Halberstam explores in *The Queer Art of Failure* as an "art of unbecoming".[24] "Our names are unknown and our faces are shadows drifting across an infinite blackness. [...]. We are the proud failures with only a single joy left to us—to inflict rampant damage on those who have fed themselves on our dreams and to choke ourselves on our own nightmares. In sum, we are expediters of the apocalypse."[25] Ligotti's vision of capitalism as apocalypse resonates with Fisher's idea of capitalist realism—the idea that capitalism is "the only viable political and economic system" and that it is "now impossible even to imagine a coherent alternative to it".[26] Fisher shares his pessimistic diagnosis with a range of thinkers such as Fredric Jameson and Slavoj Žižek, both of whom have been credited with the saying that it is easier to imagine the end of the world than it is to imagine the end of capitalism.

In Ligotti's short story, capitalism quite literally constitutes the end of the world and the solar system. Ligotti imagines this apocalypse as the result of cosmic-pessimist negation—an antidote to the destructive logic of permanent growth and expansion of corporate capitalism. In the end, Oneiricon, undermined by the failures and losers of the Nightmare Network, deteriorates into a "rotting mutation" that is ultimately awaited by the void: "The signal repeats, steadily deteriorating, and then fades into nothingness. Long shot of the universe. There is no one behind the camera."[27] By picturing the end of the universe as a cinematic staging, with no directorial authority—human, nonhuman, spiritual or otherwise—in charge, Ligotti's short story captures what he in his philosophical work describes as the titular horrific and uncanny conspiracy against the human race. In both his fiction and his philosophical text, the supernatural is the adequate mode to render the paradoxes of a "malignantly useless" existence of a species who is not in charge of its own fate.

Ligotti thus uses horror fiction's philosophical potential to think human existence. This crossover of supernatural horror and pessimist philosophy is also a central element in Ray Brassier's *Nihil Unbound* and in the work of Eugene Thacker, whose *Horror of Philosophy* trilogy makes this point most explicitly. Ligotti reads filmic narratives of alien invasion and parasitic contagion such as Philip Kaufman's *Invasion of the Body Snatchers* (1978) or John Carpenter's *The Thing* as allegories of human beings' lack of control over their own personalities, subjecthood and existence.[28] In these films, the extinction of the human species is imminent, but it is merely a logical conclusion to lives that always have been delusional "nonentities" to begin with.[29] The connection between fictions of extinction and the notion of human lives lived by something else beyond the grasp of human cognition is perhaps best illustrated in another apocalyptic film by John Carpenter, his 1994 film *In the Mouth of Madness*. The film's protagonist, the cynical private detective Trent, anticipates MacCormack's ahuman and antinatalist thinking: "Every species can smell its own extinction. The last ones left won't have a pretty time with it. In ten years, maybe less, the human race will just be a bedtime story for their children. A myth, nothing more." The irony that he cannot yet grasp in his cynicism is that he already is a myth: he is a character in a novel of horror writer Sutter Cane, a mere figment of someone else's imagination. Later, he can watch himself on the screen in the adaptation of the novel that he is a part of. Trent is a puppet of fiction, just as, according to Ligotti, all human beings are puppets in the cosmic theatre of existence.

Never masters of their own existence, equipped with what amounts to a mere illusion of subjectivity and self, then, the very notion of human life and being alive must be re-evaluated. The self—not more than a "spectral tapeworm that takes its reality from a host organism"—is characterised by its ephemeral uncanniness: "What is most uncanny about the self is that no one has yet been able to present the least evidence of it."[30] This is where Ligotti's cosmic pessimism meets the scientific nihilism of Ray Brassier, both of whom turn to German neurophilosopher Thomas Metzinger's book *Being No-One* (2004) for answers to the conundrum of self.[31] From Ligotti's cosmic-pessimist perspective, the fact that a nonentity like the human being is equipped with a consciousness that can grasp this very absurdity is yet another proof that human life is merely a grotesque aberration from the status quo of non-living. He looks to the future horizon of extinction to finally resolve this mistake: "But time will dry its eyes; time will take care of it. Time will take care of everyone until there are none of us to take care of. Then all will be as it was before we put down roots where we do not belong."[32]

In a similar vein, Ray Brassier urges his readers to take extinction as the departure for new processes of intelligibility. Extinction is real: 4.5 billion years from now, the sun will be extinguished, and life in the solar system will end. However, extinction is not empirical since "it is not of the order of experience".[33] The extinction of humans, and indeed all life, thus at first exceeds human intelligibility. Faced with the future threat of extinction, human thought and action do not only seem meaningless—they are, as Brassier argues with Lyotard, already dead even well before actual extinction takes place.[34] Thought itself is thus confronted with its own horizon of finitude: "extinction indexes the thought of the absence of thought".[35] And yet, as Brassier argues with Jean-François Lyotard's *The Inhuman*, this meaninglessness needs to be embraced.[36] Thinking the death of thought itself becomes the horizonal challenge posed by the fact of extinction. But where do we go from here? When, considering the future horizon of terrestrial extinction, everything is already dead,[37] radical possibilities for new epistemologies emerge, for philosophy itself can be recognised as the "organon of extinction" rather than a "medium of affirmation".[38] In his discussion of Brassier's work, Eugene Thacker points out that well before solar catastrophe, terrestrial species go extinct on an everyday basis (currently accelerated by anthropogenic interference) "at a 'natural background rate'".[39] The banality of (nonhuman) extinction, then, is superseded by the horizon of the extinction of all life and human thought. The very thing that is capable of thinking time in terms of past, present and future—human cognition—thus reaches its limits in thinking about the possibility of its own end. The message that "everything is dead already" thus becomes a haunting from the future that troubles human thought and being and challenges "romantic reveries of an unbounded future of human possibility and potential".[40] From a pessimist-hauntological perspective then, solar catastrophe proves to be a twofold haunting from the future.

The notion of extinction as the future horizon that determines possibility in the present also looms large in the work of ecological thinkers Timothy Morton and Patricia MacCormack. The "end of the world" that Timothy Morton refers to is brought about by hyperobjects since these dramatically question conventional ontological notions of the world from an anthropocentric perspective.[41] Is this, then, merely the end of the world as concept? Only to some degree, for Morton also suggests that "[t]he end of the world has already occurred", namely the very moment (April 1784) when James Watt introduced the steam engine and thus irrevocably changed the way humans would interact with and act on nonhuman life on planet Earth. In that way, the world as it is figured in anthropocentric apocalyptic thought, a "world-for-us" whose end spells the end of humanity, is already an obsolete notion. Thus, the worry about the potential end of the world is misguided since the correlation between humans and world must be radically rethought to adequately grasp that "the end of the world is already happening, or whether perhaps *it might already have taken place*".[42] The effect of this rethinking amounts to a drastic shift in ecological awareness (in that the direction of this awareness as a human-centric epistemological process is put into question, necessitating a new ontology) in relation to, among other hyperobjects, anthropogenic global warming.

But—and this is where Morton's thought overlaps with pessimist philosophies—it also triggers a "deep shuddering of temporality".[43] Time is not what humans thought it was, history must be rethought, and anthropocentric notions of progress must be overhauled. In challenging anthropocentric ontologies and temporalities, Morton shares similarities with pessimist thought and with theories of hauntology. His weirding of human, nonhuman and planetary time points to the recognition that "[e]cological coexistence is with ghosts, strangers, and specters precisely because of reality, not in spite of it".[44] Morton's Object-Oriented Ontology seeks to facilitate an understanding of this haunted coexistence by rethinking being beyond anthropocentric registers. It thus contributes to "radically [displacing] the human by insisting that my being is not everything it's cracked up to be—or rather that the being of a paper cup is as profound as mine".[45] Even more radically, Patricia MacCormack's approach to ecosophy does not merely seek to deprivilege humans in their exceptional status. Rather than Morton's "ecognosis"—a "weird attunement" to the uncanny fact that nonhuman elements are installed in what is thought of as the human[46]—MacCormack proposes to realise that humans act parasitically upon other life forms. Her ahuman ethics thus promotes voluntary extinction as an ethical way to "gracefully" step aside to let other life flourish.[47] MacCormack's notion of "the grace of human extinction"[48] is thus not apocalyptic in the anthropocentric sense. She thinks of the apocalypse not as a singular event but as multiple events that adhere to different teleologies rather than being just one culminating event:

> Every age has its impending apocalypse. Every arena has its intimate apocalypse. Every understanding of the present has the apocalypses upon which it reflects and those which it sees as imminent. The end of the world shows us two highly postmodern 'things'—life, time, history and existence are neither narrative nor linear, and a thing's thingness is made up of its own mythology, not empirical truth. […]. We occupy a world where the unexpected affects of anthropocentric causes, primarily industrial, evince how little we know even when we think we know.[49]

MacCormack's argument shares with Morton its de-centring of the human and its figuration of the end(s) of the world as a horizon of a new non-anthropocentric thinking, but she comes to even more radical and polemic conclusions that are in line with the absolutism of Ligottian pessimism, but not so much with Morton's calls for "ecognosis".[50]

What I hoped to show with my comparative discussion of Ligotti, Brassier, Morton and MacCormack is how the concern with human extinction as a horizon of thought unites seemingly disparate thinkers. What Morton's and MacCormack's ecological pessimisms share is a reconsideration of apocalypse to challenge (late) modernity's notions of temporality and historicity. They both try to come to terms with the temporality of what has variously been labelled the Anthropocene or the Capitalocene.[51] Their thinking in the future tense, however, comes to different conclusions. Both advocate the end of conventional categories of the human. But while Morton calls for a "logic of future coexistence", MacCormack opts for the "end as affirmation"[52] that forecloses coexistence and proposes a human stepping aside through voluntary extinction as a form of care for other lives. Both also work towards a radical ontological rethinking of the human and a deprivileging of an anthropocentric view—and this is what they have in common with Thomas Ligotti and Ray Brassier, even if these four thinkers might on the surface have different concerns and might not necessarily subscribe to each other's approaches.

A pessimist epistemology which uses extinction as the horizon of expectation can come to terms with the temporality of anthropocentric modes of living by using the future prospect of extinction as a frame to view the present. It seeks, in Morton's words, to find an "exit from modernity"[53] and its impasses by thinking the future beyond the human. A pessimist mode of critique can also shift the focus from what Eugene Thacker has called the world-for-us to the perspective of a world-without-us. It can thus come to terms with the way humans relate to the nonhuman world, particularly in the context of fossil-fuel capitalism and its impact on all forms of terrestrial life, both in terms of how such relationships are being lived in the present and in terms of what these lived relationships mean for planetary and ecological futures.

AFFIRMATION OF THE END: LARS VON TRIER'S *MELANCHOLIA*

Two cinematic representations of the end of the world can help to explore the multi-layered proposals of extinctionist philosophies. Lars von Trier's *Melancholia* (2011) and Camille Griffin's *Silent Night* (2021) are examples of that rare kind of apocalyptic narrative in which the end of humanity is not averted. Other examples include John Carpenter's loosely connected "Apocalypse Trilogy" *The Thing* (1982), *Prince of Darkness* (1987) and *In the Mouth of Madness* (1994) or, from the same year as *Melancholia*, Abel Ferrara's *4:44: Last Day on Earth* (2011). All of these films are prime examples of philosophically pessimist films (Carpenter's emulation of cosmic horror being the closest to Ligotti's pessimism), but I want to focus on von Trier and Griffin's films since they are striking examples of the twenty-first-century conjuncture of pessimism I outlined in this book. What is more, they most clearly point to the challenge to reconcile extinctionist philosophies with the concerns of cultural studies.

In Lars von Trier's *Melancholia*, the main character Justine embraces the end of the world and what Thacker calls cosmic pessimism's "uncanny zone of passivity", a "letting be".[54] Justine's letting be, like Ligotti's anti-corporation of losers, might be the result of her clinically depressed disposition, but in the context of the film's aesthetic and philosophical strategies, her failure to "function" in a socially acceptable way amounts to a negation of the cynical logic of capital represented by her boss Jack and her brother-in-law, John. Justine suffers from severe depression which, halfway through the film, becomes more and more debilitating. The first half of the film focusses on Justine's wedding. Her wealthy yet dysfunctional family has made every effort to make it the perfect wedding celebration. This part of the film is a comedy of manners which lays bare absurd social rituals. It becomes clear that Justine's family is trying to manage her depression by forcing her to be happy. As her rich brother-in-law angrily tells her, they had a "deal" that he pays for the wedding, and in turn, she has to be (or at least act) happy. In von Trier's bleak but comedic vision of human relationships under capitalism, even affect and emotional attachment have become subject to the logic of the market. Feelings have become yet another matter of trade and exchange value. Meanwhile, Justine's boss Jack has ordered her, his best employee, to come up with the tagline for a new product by the end of her wedding night. Tim, Jack's nephew and new intern, is tasked with following Justine during the festivities to be there the moment inspiration strikes. This story arc seems like an illustration of Theodor Adorno's bleak observation that under modern capitalism, "the forms of the production process are repeated in private life [...] the whole of life must look like a job, and by this resemblance conceal what is not yet directly devoted to pecuniary gain".[55] The wedding ceremony is thus rendered as the ultimate form of capitalist debt: Justine owes her family and her boss, thus trapped in a corporate logic even during what is supposed to be her happiest moment.

Why does von Trier's film—a film ostensibly about depression and the end of the world—spend its first half on Justine's failed wedding? After all, a lavishly choreographed and styled prelude, set to Richard Wagner's Tristan und Isolde, already served as a prolepsis of the inevitable end, rendering the apocalypse almost obscenely gorgeous, and the last part of the film goes back to this style, offering lush imagery of the last moments of Earth.[56] The first part seems like a digression, with a varied ensemble of characters played by prominent actors being introduced and then dropped as the film moves into its second half. Von Trier is not exclusively concerned with character building here, even if he provides a nuanced portrayal of Justine and how she navigates interpersonal encounters. What is equally if not more interesting, however, is how the backdrop to Justine's absurd wedding is the economic and monetary entanglement implied in the proceedings. Happiness can seemingly be bought if someone is willing to pay the right amount. The film, then, can be read in the context of Mark Fisher's concept of capitalist realism which, as he points out early on in his book, is based on the "phrase attributed to Fredric Jameson and Slavoj Žižek, that it is easier to imagine the end of the world than it is to imagine the end of capitalism. That slogan captures precisely what I mean by 'capitalist realism': the widespread sense that not only is capitalism the only viable political and economic system, but also that it is now impossible even to imagine a coherent alternative to it."[57] What better way out of this impasse, then, than to embrace the end of the world as an end to the nihilist capitalist logic that has hollowed out human relationships and is devastating the planet anyway? This suicidal logic, which is both an affective and an ethical one, is at the heart of *Melancholia*'s extinctionist imagination.

Von Trier's perspective on capitalism as an all-pervading principle resonates with Schopenhauer's thesis that human existence itself "has entirely the character of a contracted *debt*".[58] Justine opposes this oppressive logic by willfully crashing her own wedding (which was never "her" wedding in the first place). She confronts Jack with his toxic narcissism: "what if instead we try and sell you to the public, Jack? Well then, surprisingly, I'd arrive right back where I started from—at nothing". Tim suggests that "nothing" is "not such a bad tagline".[59] The scene exemplifies the power of pessimist negation which exposes the emptiness of capitalism's signifiers and exchange value. The night ends with her cynical boss firing her, her husband-to-be leaving her, and her co-dependent sister realising how utterly trivial their attachment to social ritual really is.

It is only in the face of imminent apocalypse that Justine's depression lifts: her whole life of illness has prepared her for the end, while her arrogant scientist brother-in-law kills himself once he realises that the scientists were a bit too optimistic about the planet Melancholia passing Earth by. Justine's "letting be" and embracing of extinction becomes an ethical stance. As she tells her sister, "the Earth is evil. We don't need to grieve for it [...] life on Earth is evil", and therefore will not be missed in the cosmic scheme of things.[60] Justine's statement that "life on Earth is evil" echoes both Schopenhauer's scepticism about life as a "desirable state"[61] and Ligotti's characterisation of sentient life as a malignant state. But it goes even beyond MacCormack's misanthropy. MacCormack's apocalyptic thinking only subjects the human species to an ethical judgement, *Melancholia*'s philosophy renders life as a cosmic accident that is inherently and fundamentally evil, irrespective of species. Justine, and with her the film, offers a vision of the "end as affirmation" (MacCormack) and therefore a pessimism in the Schopenhauerian sense as a cosmic, "impersonal attitude".[62]

Justine's position is, as Joshua Foa Dienstag has argued, an ethical one. Her "pessimist realism" exposes the capitalist nihilism of her boss and the delusions of her sister and her brother-in-law, all of which amount to a "world-blindness" that Justine, in the final hours, meets first with ruthless realism and then with compassion as she nurses her nephew in the moments of planetary death.[63] Justine's ethical stance, Dienstag argues, also raises questions of representation. Justine's pessimist clear-sightedness points to the representability of evil in the world—something which her sister is blind to—in order to have an adequate representation of the world. However, Justine's indictment of the Earth and all life on it as evil might have even deeper implications about the representability of the world and life as such. Justine's statements are in stark contrast to the sheer visual spectacle with which von Trier renders the world about to fatally collide with the planet Melancholia. One is reminded of Schopenhauer, who pointed out that the supposed beauty the world has to offer humanity's aesthetic gaze does not adequately represent being the world: "an optimist tells me to open my eyes and look at the world and see how beautiful it is in the sunshine, with its mountains, valleys, rivers, plants, animals and so on. But is the world then a peep-show? These things are certainly beautiful to *behold*, but to *be* them is something quite different."[64] Justine's no-saying to the world, then, could in Schopenhauerian terms be a no-saying to the world as a mere representation, as a world-for-us.

Taking the Exit: Camille Griffin's *Silent Night*

"I've seen *The Road,* and there's no fucking way I'm living like that—I can't do postapocalyptic monochrome", wails Bella, one of the dinner guests who have met at a country estate to prepare for the imminent apocalypse in Camille Griffin's *Silent Night.*[65] An unspecified ecological disaster has caused a devastating poisonous gas storm that will gradually engulf the earth and kill most life on the planet. The poison cloud is expected to hit Britain the night before Christmas, and the government has provided "exit pills" allowing all citizens "to avoid suffering and [to] die with dignity", as the public service announcement soothingly promises.[66] That the end of the world is, among many other concerns, also an aesthetic problem for Bella, points to the film's overt meta-awareness about (post-)apocalyptic narratives and their conventions. For the most part, the film plays very much like the first half of von Trier's *Melancholia*. Its social comedy of manners riffs on the quirks of the posh family gathering at the estate. Nell and her husband Simon, the hosts of the night, are adamant that appearances are kept up despite the impending doom, the only exception being that the children are, for once, allowed to swear and drink a late-night coke to wash down their exit pill. Nell, Simon and their extended family and friends have made a pact to take their exit pills together to avoid a painful death by poison gas.

Like Lars von Trier, Camille Griffin is interested in how the values and principles of everyday human life under capitalism clash with the reality of extinction. While von Trier uses his main character Justine as a mouthpiece for a depressive-pessimist realism who iconoclastically confronts others with her truth claims and tells her sister Claire that her plan to make the best of the apocalypse by sharing some wine is "a piece of shit",[67] in *Silent Night* it is Nell and Simon's little son Art and pregnant Sophie, the young wife of one of Simon's friends, who voice their dissent and do not accept the suggested proceedings. However, whereas Justine accepts and in fact welcomes the end of the world, Art and Sophie are appalled at the dominant acceptance of the government's euthanasia measures. If Art and Sophie can be called pessimists at all (after all, both hold on to the unlikely possibility that the expected environmental disaster might be survivable and that there might be a livable future worth fighting for, not least for Sophie's unborn baby), theirs is less Justine's (and von Trier's) cosmic pessimism, but a political pessimism. According to Thacker's typology, Art and Sophie could be labelled moral pessimists in their "no-saying to the worst".[68] Theirs is a pessimism born out of a profound scepticism towards authorities and the desperate question whether all options have been exhausted. Both Sophie and Art are, as it were, philosophical outsiders within the family. Sophie's perspective is informed by her emotions as a newly pregnant woman, but also by her class status: when she and her husband James arrive at the party, she is anxious about the unwritten rules of conduct at his friends' house: "posh people always have secrets!" Throughout the night, Art confronts the adults with their decisions and questionable values. Echoing climate activist Greta Thunberg's address at the 2019 UN Climate Summit, Art blames his parents' generation for causing or at least not actively preventing the environmental crisis that will culminate in the oncoming toxic storm: "You've all fucked it up—it's a disaster!"[69] By repeatedly referring to the situation as a "disaster", Art does not mean the impending catastrophe, but the overall situation that brought it about in the first place. Like Timothy Morton and Patricia MacCormack, Art identifies the time of disaster and the end of the world not as a future moment (even if that future moment might be the very next morning) but as a process that has been going on for quite some time. The temporality of the end of the world, of extinction, is one of duration.

The film's script emphasises the nuances of temporality and duration. Arriving at the Christmas party for one last night of fun, the participants simultaneously know full well that they're already dead even while their imminent extinction is not yet of the order of their experience. When Nell exclaims, "we're all getting old", her friend James, corrects her, "we *were* getting old!"[70] James is a cancer doctor and therefore has a firmer grasp on human finitude than most adults present, but even for him, it is mostly an abstract medical fact. As in *Melancholia*, the apocalypse takes place within the symbolic-representational regime of capitalism. When Sandra parades her expensive party outfit, her daughter points out that "you're wearing my education on your feet!" The way the parent generation—in this case a group of upper-class characters, not all of which seem to be able to handle their money responsibly ("I'm worth nothing", Bella says at some point)—uses the apocalypse as (yet another) opportunity to squander their income seems suspicious to their children. Even though some of them accept their fate more sheepishly than Art, they still cannot help but question their parents' motives. Art's parents keep reaffirming that they just want the kids to be happy and that providing them with exit pills is an act of mercy. It does not escape the children that it is an absurd thing to say in the face of extinction.

In Chap. 4, I elaborated on Lee Edelman and Sara Ahmed's queer pessimism as an intervention into the temporal logic of "reproductive futurism". In *Silent Night*, it seems that even in the face of the apocalypse, the "Child remains the perpetual horizon of every acknowledged politics, the fantasmatic beneficiary of every political intervention"[71]—which does not mean that politics are particularly concerned with actual children, but with the figure of the Child as a projection of cultural and political normativity. Consequently, the adults in Griffin's film appear like spoiled children who in their emotional and moral immaturity demand their children to fulfil their political and emotional projections. Sandra forcing her daughter to give her a hug because she "deserves" it is a case in point that demonstrates the emotionally needy parents' desire to project their narcissism onto their children. Meanwhile, Art demands the adults to take responsibility for what is about to happen. "As your parents we're not to blame", is his mother's reply.[72] His parents tell him that "there is no alternative" to taking the pill—an echo of former Conservative Prime Minister Margaret Thatcher's dictum that "there is no alternative" to free-market economics, which for Mark Fisher is the epitome of the representational logic of "capitalist realism".[73]

Capitalist realism, as what cultural studies have theorised with Louis Althusser as systems of representation to analyse how people form imaginary relations with their social reality,[74] seems to be intact, and in *Silent Night*, it perversely even seems to transcend the end of the world. The adults are caught up in this ideological representational framing. It is the perspective of the sceptical child, however, which challenges the "impossibilism"[75] and demands to know about who is excluded from representation, and therefore from view. When he learns that some people—the homeless and illegal immigrants—have not been given the exit pill because "according to the government they don't legally exist", he is morally appalled. The film's bleak conclusion, then, is that even death and the end of the world do not turn out to be the great leveller and that even in the moment of extinction, class inequality and racism persist. Not everyone is equal to dignified death at the end of the world. Even if the human species mourns itself in the future tense, there are, to paraphrase Judith Butler, grievable and less grievable lives, and those precarious lives excluded from or victimised by hegemonic relations do not get to enjoy the apocalypse equally.[76] The child character Art, then, functions as an admonishing commenter who exposes the ideological imaginaries of his complacent and self-centred parents and their friends. His provocative questions are formulated in the mode of critique in line with the central concerns of cultural studies: the symbolic and political aspects of representational regimes and how these intersect with ideological hegemony. His rhetoric is the rhetoric of moral and political pessimism, aimed at the parent generation. But the film's pessimism even goes beyond the child's critique by suggesting that even extinction—which, according to Ray Brassier is not of the order of human experience, can only be experienced within the representational system of capitalist realism.

Ahuman Futures

Melancholia and *Silent Night* prefigure futures not only after the human but after earth. It imagines an end to the entire planet. Even if extinction is not of the "order of experience",[77] apocalyptic narratives at least aesthetically attempt to make it knowable. These narratives create a pessimist epistemological frame through which a "world-without-us"[78] beyond and after the human can be conceived. They explode the cruelly optimistic attachments and investments into the human of the Capitalocene and the Anthropocene by radically de-realising capitalist realism. It is in this intervention into anthropocentric and capital-driven notions of "hope" and "optimism" that the potential of cosmic pessimism can be fully explored. For even if, as Eugene Thacker argues, cosmic pessimism is not so much a philosophy as an anti-philosophy, it can still perform something as a thought. Its force of negation opens up imaginative possibilities that, from the point of view of neoliberal optimisation and capitalist productivity, might seem unproductive, or, more accurately, anti-productive. Cosmic pessimism renders humanity as an afterthought: it offers a futurity that rejects the notion of modernity and human progress and thinks the world after the human (or the cosmos after earth, see Ligotti and von Trier). It thus explodes capitalism's "unreality" and its cruel optimism by letting go of such illusions. In that, cosmic pessimism shares sensibilities with the field of hauntology. Both are concerned with thinking the present as haunted by traces of the past and of futures that were not yet and might never be. The cosmic-pessimist imagination goes a step further by thinking a future in which the entire human species will merely be a spectral trace.

What the apocalyptic narratives compared in this chapter demonstrate is that pessimism is ambivalent and relational. Being pessimistic about the sustainability of human civilisation and its impact on other ecosystems and the planet can be a pessimism about the future of the human species from an anthropocentric perspective. It can also be pessimistic about the future survival of other, nonhuman species. But it can also be cheerfully and paradoxically optimistic, rejecting the anthropocentric view in favour of a perspective that affirms other species and can be optimistic about the positive effects of the demise of one's own species for the benefit of others. This attitude in itself, epitomised in MacCormack's "end as affirmation", can be troubling depending on one's own perspective and value system. Such an attitude can have an eeriness about itself that results from the counter-intuitive rejection of solidarity with one's own species. This is a perspective that invites humans to perceive the world beyond themselves, possibility beyond (human) life—a future in which humans as a species are merely ghosts.

NOTES

1. Thomas Ligotti, *The Conspiracy against the Human Race: A Contrivance of Horror* (New York: Hippocampus Press, 2010), p. 47.
2. Ligotti, 2010, p. 47.
3. Ligotti, 2010, pp. 47–48.
4. Ligotti, 2010, p. 48.
5. Ligotti, 2010, p. 4.
6. Eugene Thacker, *Starry Speculative Corpse: Horror of Philosophy Vol. 2* (Winchester: Zero, 2015a), p. 142.
7. Eugene Thacker, *Cosmic Pessimism* (Minneapolis: Univocal, 2015c), p. 12.
8. Eugene Thacker, *After Life* (Chicago: The University of Chicago Press, 2010), p. 268.
9. MacCormack, 2020, p. 11.
10. Patricia MacCormack, *The Ahuman Manifesto: Activism for the End of the Anthropocene* (New York: Bloomsbury, 2020), pp. 171–172.
11. MacCormack, 2020, p. 172.
12. For one, Patricia MacCormack has voiced her ambivalence about pessimism as a masculinist gesture, cf. Joseph Packer and Ethan Stoneman, *A Feeling of Wrongness: Pessimistic Rhetoric on the Fringes of Popular Culture* (University Park: Penn State University Press, 2018), p. 18.
13. Franco "Bifo" Berardi, *After the Future* (Edinburgh: AK Press, 2011).
14. MacCormack, 2020.
15. Thacker, 2010.
16. Admittedly, as Eugene Thacker rightly observes, describing *The Conspiracy Against the Human Race* as a strictly philosophical book in the academic sense would not do it justice. In his discussion of the book, Thacker makes important remarks about the style of the book, which can be at times essayistic, at times scholarly discussion, at times lyrical prose and that it "constantly hovers around that boundary between writing *about* pessimism and simply *writing* pessimism" (*Tentacles Longer Than Night: Horror of Philosophy Vol. 3* (Winchester: Zero, 2015b), p. 158). Thus, it would perhaps be more accurate to describe Ligotti's book in performative terms. It does not think about pessimism, it *performs* it.
17. Ligotti, 2010, p. 227.

18. Ligotti, 2010, p. 205.
19. Thomas Ligotti, "The Nightmare Network", in *My Work Is Not Yet Done: Three Tales of Corporate Horror* (London: Virgin Books, 2009), 169–190, p. 175.
20. Ligotti, 2009, p. 171.
21. Ligotti, 2009, pp. 181–182.
22. Scott Sandage, *Born Losers: A History of Failure in America* (Cambridge: Harvard University Press, 2005), p. 9.
23. Cf. J. Jack Halberstam, *The Queer Art of Failure* (Durham: Duke University Press, 2011).
24. Halberstam, 2011, p. 88.
25. Ligotti, 2009, pp. 175–176.
26. Fisher, 2009, p. 2.
27. Ligotti, 2009, p. 183.
28. Ligotti, 2010, pp. 90–93.
29. Ligotti, 2010, p. 105.
30. Ligotti, 2010, p. 101.
31. Cf. Ligotti, 2010, pp. 105–113; Ray Brassier, *Nihil Unbound: Enlightenment and Extinction* (Basingstoke: Palgrave, 2007), pp. 29, 31. See also Graham Harman's criticism of Metzinger's approach and Brassier's use of it in *Speculative Realism: An Introduction* (Cambridge: Polity, 2020), pp. 20–21.
32. Ligotti, 2010, p. 227.
33. Brassier, 2007, p. 238.
34. Brassier, 2007, p. 223.
35. Brassier, 2007, pp. 229–230.
36. Cf. Brassier, 2007, pp. 238–239.
37. Cf. Brasier, 2007, p. 223 and Jean-François Lyotard, *The Inhuman: Reflections on Time* (Cambridge: Polity Press, 1993), p. 9.
38. Brassier, 2007, p. 239.
39. Thacker, 2015a, p. 159.
40. Thacker, 2015a, p. 160.
41. Timothy Morton, *Hyperobjects: Philosophy and Ecology after the End of the World* (Minneapolis, London: University of Minnesota Press, 2013), pp. 6–7.
42. Morton 2013, p. 16.
43. Morton, 2013, p. 16.
44. Morton, 2013, p. 195.
45. Morton, 2013, p. 17.
46. Timothy Morton, *Dark Ecology: For a Logic of Future Coexistence* (New York: Columbia University Press, 2016), p. 159.
47. Patricia MacCormack, "The Ahuman", in *The Bloomsbury Handbook of Posthumanism* (London: Bloomsbury, 2020), 71–79.

48. Patricia MacCormack, "The Grace of Extinction", in *Michel Serres and the Crises of the Contemporary*, ed. Rick Dolphijn (London: Bloomsbury, 2019), 147–68.
49. MacCormack, 2020, p. 171.
50. Morton, 2016, p. 159.
51. For a discussion of both concepts, see Jason W. Moore, *Anthropocene or Capitalocene? Nature, History, and the Crisis of Capitalism* (Oakland: PM Press, 2016).
52. MacCormack, 2020 p. 1.
53. Morton, 2016, p. 146.
54. Thacker, 2015a, p. 140.
55. Theodor Adorno, *Minima Moralia: Reflections from Damaged Life* (London: Verso, 2020), p. 148.
56. Joshua Foa Dienstag has argued that the visual excess and lush stylisation of the prelude and the last part of *Melancholia* are the antithesis of Lars von Trier's former Dogme 95 realist and cinema verité style, as if to subvert his own aesthetic principles of filmmaking, cf. Joshua Foa Dienstag, *Cinema Pessimism: A Political Theory of Representation and Reciprocity* (Oxford: Oxford University Press, 2020), p. 96.
57. Mark Fisher, *Capitalist Realism. Is There No Alternative?* (Winchester: Zero, 2009), p. 2.
58. Arthur Schopenhauer, *On the Suffering of the World*, ed. Eugene Thacker (London: Repeater, 2020), p. 76.
59. *Melancholia,* directed by Lars von Trier (Zentropa / Nordisk Film, 2011).
60. *Melancholia,* 2011.
61. Schopenhauer, 2020, p. 83.
62. Thacker, 2015a, p. 127.
63. Dienstag, 2020, p. 105.
64. Schopenhauer, 2020, p. 78, emphasis in original.
65. *Silent Night,* directed by Camille Griffin (Altitude, 2021).
66. *Silent Night,* 2021.
67. *Melancholia,* 2011.
68. Thacker, 2015c, p. 12.
69. *Silent Night,* 2021.
70. *Silent Night,* 2021.
71. Lee Edelman, *No Future: Queer Theory and the Death Drive* (Durham: Duke University Press, 2004), p. 3.
72. *Silent Night,* 2021.
73. Fisher, 2009, p. 8.
74. See Stuart Hall, *Cultural Studies 1983: A Theoretical History* (Durham: Duke University Press, 2016), pp. 135–137.

75. John Storey, *Radical Utopianism and Cultural Studies: On Refusing to Be Realistic* (Abingdon: Routledge, 2019), p. 7. See also chapter 2 for my discussion of John Storey's utopianism.
76. See Judith Butler, *Precarious Life: The Powers of Mourning and Violence* (London: Verso, 2006).
77. Brassier, 2007, p. 238.
78. Thacker, 2015c, p. 12.

Conclusion: Cultural Studies, Prefigurative Thought and the (Ab)Uses of Pessimism

Abstract The conclusion reflects on the insights that the analyses of the philosophical, political and cultural texts in this book have provided and makes suggestions for the future place of pessimism in cultural studies. Pessimism will continue to haunt culture in times of overly optimistic hopes for solutions to the social, political and ecological problems of the current conjuncture. The concluding chapter takes Lawrence Grossberg's proposals for a "cultural studies in the future tense" as the starting point for its discussion of the relationship between cultural studies and pessimism. Given that cultural studies are often understood as an intellectual project with emancipatory political aims, it might be counterintuitive to engage with a form of thought that most would consider to be "unconstructive" and negative. The chapter offers an argument for pessimism as a mode to reflect on the epistemologies and knowledges of cultural studies.

Keywords Cultural studies • Future • Epistemology • Knowledge • Hauntology • Lawrence Grossberg

The new pessimisms haunting the current conjuncture are hard to ignore. They expose and respond to the multiple crises of the present from the ills of capitalism to racism, sexism, homophobia, speciesism and climate disaster. Strands like queer pessimism, antinatalism, afropessimism and ecopessimism echo the particularities and contingencies of the contemporary

M. Schmitt, *Spectres of Pessimism*,
https://doi.org/10.1007/978-3-031-25351-5

world. Thus, these pessimisms address questions which are also at the heart of contemporary cultural studies. If, as Lawrence Grossberg contends, cultural studies—as an intellectual project that is concerned with analysing the present as much as with thinking about the future—must find ways to describe "the unbecoming and rebecoming [...] of modernities, the possibility of other modernities" to understand the present,[1] then it must also seriously consider these new pessimisms. As I have argued throughout this book, pessimist thought radically questions notions of temporality in ways that resemble the tenets of hauntology. This means that it disrupts linear notions of time and progress and challenges human time-consciousness. Pessimism, as the "doppelgänger" of progress,[2] can tell the story of a different modernity, and it is a story that cultural studies should take into consideration. In this book, I have offered readings of cultural texts that either perform such pessimist disruptions of time by deconstructing the representation of time and imagining other times and futures beyond the human or can be read against the grain from a pessimist perspective. In these readings, pessimist thought has proven to be a complex form of epistemology and prefiguration.

However, if, as many scholars such as Stuart Hall, Lawrence Grossberg and John Storey do, cultural studies is considered to be an academic endeavour that is not only concerned with the analysis and interpretation of cultural phenomena and texts but as a comprehensive critical study of the intersection and reciprocal relationship of these phenomena with social, political and ideological formations—and is therefore to some degree political itself—then pessimism might pose a problem. Some who subscribe to a view of cultural studies as a scholarly project that is undertaken with the "obligation to leave the world a better place"[3] might have misgivings about engaging seriously with a body of thought that barely if ever offers constructive solutions. Pessimism might share with cultural studies its scepticism about hegemony and ideology, but is it suited to make the world a better place? How, for example, can the Marxism of some versions of cultural studies be reconciled with the life-negating outlook of cosmic pessimism or the misanthropy of some antinatalist thinkers? Some might say that it is not politically constructive to dwell on the meaninglessness of life and that it could even be potentially reactionary to suggest that humanity is incapable of changing for the better. Conversely, some of the pessimist thinkers discussed in the previous chapters might object to potential attempts of being utilised for such a project of cultural studies and their absolutist radicalism being diluted in the process. To paraphrase Sara Ahmed and Thomas Ligotti, such a utilisation of pessimist thought for making the world a better place through cultural theorising would not only be naïve (a yes-saying to something that should not be in the first place) but also mean being too optimistic about pessimism.

So how does the future- and hope-oriented disposition of such a version of cultural studies react to the no-saying of pessimism? There are several answers to this question. Pessimism—and the new pessimisms of the current conjuncture in particular—in many ways already addresses core concerns of cultural studies. These include the construction of social and political identities, the study of representation as a symbolic and material practice and how these produce and reflect on how identities are being made and lived. Afropessimism, for instance, is a radical epistemological reframing of the way Black identities are rendered in societies shaped by white hegemony and the history of slavery. It is a pessimism that is sceptical about easy representational fixes. Similarly, a pessimist perspective can offer critical insights into the relationship of cultural representations of groups, individuals and their identities and what this means for their representation in the arena of democratic politics.[4] Pessimism, then, can function as a corrective to overly optimistic (and daresay naïve) inflections of cultural studies.

But this, again, might be read as reducing pessimism to its "use value"—micro-dosing pessimism as a corrective to ensure the proper functioning of cultural studies: we do want some pessimism, but only a little bit, commensurable—so as not to get our hands dirty. This might run the risk of becoming the academic equivalent of "pop pessimism" and its "solutionism".[5]

What if, however, cultural studies confront pessimism as that which always resists? I want to return once more to Lawrence Grossberg's proposals for "cultural studies in the future tense". Describing the "ethical responsibility of the intellectual", Grossberg identifies the "never-ending effort to belong with the other" as the major aim of intellectual activity in the context of cultural studies.[6] This "belonging together with the other" is something which "can only be imagined", and can be "a coming community, a planetary humanity, or even as 'the earth'".[7] It is for this being with the other that the intellectual has an "obligation to imagine an other [sic] world".[8] This imagining of the other and of a better world is, for Grossberg, the core of an ethical practice of care. Considering that many strands of pessimist thought are ultimately about a rethinking of ethics, eudaemonia and compassion in recognition of the suffering of sentient beings, one can see some overlaps of Grossberg's idealistic vision and a pessimist ethics. At the same time, however, Grossberg's emphasis on the unknowability of the other points to a pessimist epistemology. Pessimism, then, could be about this other—it could, in terms of intelligibility, even *be* this other: the other as that which resists and which keeps the imagination of being with the other in a permanent state of suspension.

If cultural studies wants to be relevant as a prefigurative mode of theorising and analysis, then it must also be ready to test the limits—and even the possible end—of thought. What has emerged from the readings undertaken in this book is the way pessimism articulates a grieving for the future. Whether it is the (no-)future of the unborn child, the (no-)future and the being stuck in the present of Black and queer bodies and subjects, or the death of species, the Earth and even the universe—pessimism, like hauntology, points to the lost futures taking effect in the present in a gesture of grief. Working through this abject grief and turning it into a productive process of mourning[9]—a mourning as care for (lost) futures—could be the goal of prefigurative cultural studies. For this, cultural theory must be ready for the end of thought, the end of knowledge and the end of the world.

Thus, pessimism could account for "a set of crises around the very authority of 'knowledge'" that Grossberg identifies in contemporary cultural studies.[10] If cultural studies stands for "theory as muddle" and "multiple vision"[11] rather than a closed system of thought, then pessimism can account for the unknown, the epistemological failures and fragmentations that constitute points of resistance within the theoretical structures of cultural studies. If the theorising of cultural studies, especially in Grossberg's emphasis on imagining "better" worlds, is concerned with meaning, then it might do well to not ignore pessimism's negation of meaning. Thus, even the most radical forms of pessimist thought—cosmic and extinctionist—can offer new horizons for imagining oneself with the other. Pessimism's insistence on de-centring the human world-for-us and on thinking a world-without-us[12] can offer entirely different perspectives on this encounter with the other.